Global Complexity

GLOBAL COMPLEXITY

JOHN URRY

polity

Copyright © John Urry 2003

The right of John Urry to be identified as author of this work has been asserted in accordance with the UK Copyright, Designs and Patents Act 1988.

First published in 2003 by Polity Press in association with Blackwell Publishing Ltd.

Reprinted 2004, 2005

Polity Press
65 Bridge Street
Cambridge CB2 1UR, UK

Polity Press
350 Main Street
Malden, MA 02148, USA

A CIP catalogue record for this book is available from the British Library.

Library of Congress Cataloging-in-Publication Data

Urry, John.
  Global complexity / John Urry.
    p. cm.
  Includes bibliographical references and index.
  ISBN 0-7456-2817-6 (hbk.) – ISBN 0-7456-2818-4 (pbk.)
  1. Globalization. 2. International relations. 3. Social systems. I. Title.

JZ1249 .U77 2003
327.1'01'1857—dc21   2002072082

Typeset in 11 on 13 pt Berling
by SNP Best-set Typesetter Ltd., Hong Kong
Printed and bound in Great Britain by MPG Digital Solutions, Bodmin, Cornwall

For further information on Polity, visit our website: http://www.polity.co.uk

Everything flows.

Heraclitus

Time is not absolutely defined.

Albert Einstein

We are observing the birth of a science that is no longer limited to idealized and simplified situations but reflects the complexity of the real world, a science that views us and our creativity as part of the fundamental trend present at all levels of nature.

Ilya Prigogine

Elements are elements only for the system that employs them as units and they are such only through this system.

Niklas Luhmann

We are but whirlpools in a river of ever-flowing water.

Norbert Wiener

If you want to humble an empire it makes sense to maim its cathedrals. They are symbols of its faith, and when they crumple and burn, it tells us we are not so powerful and we can't be safe.

Time Magazine, 12 September 2001

Contents

Preface

During the 1990s, like many others, I became fascinated by the idea that social relations are in some sense increasingly global. In *The Tourist Gaze* in 1990 I briefly considered how many different places had to compete on a more global stage in order to attract tourists from all sorts of other places (Urry 1990, 2001). Later works, such as *Consuming Places* (Urry 1995), brought out how people across the world's stage are global consumers of other places and that this very importantly changes what places are like. They are on the world's stage.

More generally, Scott Lash and I analysed such global transformations through the 'end of organized capitalism' thesis. Capitalism, we argued, is shifting from an organized national, societal pattern, to global 'disorganization' (Lash and Urry 1987, 1994). In *Economies of Signs and Space* (Lash and Urry 1994) we showed that moving rapidly in and across the world are complex and mobile economies, both of signs *and* of people working in, escaping from or seduced by various signs. These signs and people increasingly flow along various 'scapes', resulting in further 'disorganization' of once organized capitalist societies. It was claimed that there is a move from the 'social' to the informational and communicational, from national government to global disorganization. Such a mobile economy of signs produces complex redrawings of the boundaries of what is global and what is local. We tried to elaborate some of the time and space changes involved in what Roland Robertson had termed 'glocalization'.

Later in the decade Phil Macnaghten and I maintained that there is no such simple entity as 'nature' (Macnaghten and Urry 1998). There is nothing 'natural', we showed, about nature. There are a variety of *Contested Natures* and one of these could be termed 'global nature'. We explored the emergence of what Ulrich Beck has described as a 'global risk society', especially describing in detail the international ramifications of the sad story of the British cow, roast beef, BSE and new variant CJD.

This led me in *Sociology beyond Societies* (Urry 2000b) to try to rethink the very bases of sociology. I showed there, following Manuel Castells's trilogy on *The Information Age* (1996, 1997, 1998), that the emergence of global networks transforms the very nature of social life. It can no longer be seen as bounded within national societies. The concept of society is revealed to be deeply problematic, once the scale, range and depth of various mobile and global processes are examined. I suggested that such transformations lead us to rethink the nature of sociology, which had been mostly based upon attempts to understand the properties and reproduction of 'societies'. I elaborated some 'new rules of sociological method' to deal with disorganization, global flows and the declining powers of the 'social'.

However, in all these works, I, like most other commentators, did not sufficiently examine the nature of the 'global' that was supposedly making great changes to social life and undermining 'societies'. The global was almost left as a 'black box', a deus ex machina that in and of itself was seen to have powerful properties. What was not analysed I think by anyone much was just what sort of 'system' the global is. Thus there was a rather weak understanding of how the systemic properties of the global interact with the properties of other entities such as those of 'society'. The global is often taken to be both the 'cause' of immense changes and the 'effect' of those changes.

As I was completing *Sociology beyond Societies* I became increasingly aware of the growth within certain of the social sciences of some concepts and theories from the complexity sciences. This is over and beyond economics, where complexity was initially developed (see Arthur 1994b). I tried to develop some elements of complexity in *Sociology beyond Societies*, especially in relationship to thinking through how time and space are transformed in a globalizing world. But more recently this small stream of complexity thinking in the social sciences has been turning into a flood. In this current book I have tried to draw on some elements in a more systematic way, although I am well aware of the dangers of crass simplification and misunderstanding as disciplinary boundaries get crossed. My formulations are qualitative, with no attempts to apply the mathematics of chaos and complexity.

The social science of globalization had taken the global *system* for granted and then shown how localities, regions, nation states, environments and cultures are transformed in linear fashion by this all-powerful 'globalization'. Thus globalization (or global capitalism) has come to be viewed as the new 'structure', with nations, localities, regions and so on, the new 'agent', employing the normal social science distinctions but given a kind of global twist.

But complexity would suggest that such a system would be diverse, historical, fractured and uncertain. It would be necessary to examine how emergent properties develop at the global level that are neither well ordered and moving towards equilibrium nor in a state of perpetual anarchy. Complexity would lead one to see the global as neither omnipotent nor subject to control by society. Indeed, it is not a single centre of power. It is an astonishingly complex system, or rather a series of dynamic complex systems, a huge array of islands of order within a sea of disorder, as Ilya Prigogine more generally postulates. There would be no presumption of moving towards a state of equilibrium.

And, as I was finishing this book, the tragic events of both 11 September and its bloody aftermath showed the profound limitations of any linear view of the global. These events demonstrate that globalization is never complete. It is disordered, full of paradox and the unexpected. Racing across the world are complex mobile connections that are more or less intense, more or less social, more or less 'networked' and more or less occurring 'at a distance'. There is a complex world, unpredictable yet irreversible, fearful and violent, disorderly but not simply anarchic. Small events in such systems are not forgotten but can reappear at different and highly unexpected points in time and space. I suggest that the way to think these notions through is via the concept of global complexity.

And in thinking through what might be meant by 'global complexity', I have been helped by various colleagues, especially Fritjof Capra, Bülent Diken, Mick Dillon, Andy Hoskins, Bob Jessop, Scott Lash, John Law, Will Medd, Mimi Sheller, Jackie Stacey, Nigel Thrift and Sylvia Walby.

John Urry
Lancaster

1

'Societies' and the Global

Introducing the Global

It increasingly seems that we are living through some extraordinary times involving massive changes to the very fabric of normal economic, political and social life. Analogies have been drawn with a century or more ago, when a somewhat similar restructuring of the dimensions of time and space took place. New technological and organizational innovations 'compressed' the time taken to communicate and travel across large distances. Some of these momentous innovations that changed time-space a century ago included the telegram, the telephone, steamship travel, the bicycle, cars and lorries, skyscrapers, aircraft, the mass production factory, X-ray machines and Greenwich Mean Time (see Kern 1983). Together these technological and social innovations dramatically reorganized and compressed the very dimensions of time and space between people and places.

Today some rather similar changes seem to be occurring. The 1990s saw the growth of the Internet with a take-up faster than any previous technology. There will soon be 1 billion users worldwide. The dealings of foreign exchange that occur each day are worth $1.4 trillion, which is sixty times greater than the amount of world trade. Communications 'on the move' are being transformed, with new mobile phones now more common in the world than conventional land-line phones. There are 700 million international journeys made each year, a figure predicted to pass 1 billion very soon. Microsoft pointedly asks: 'where do you want to go today?' and there are many ways of getting 'there'.

At the same time tens of millions of refugees and asylum-seekers roam the globe, with three billion people across the world receiving the same total income as the richest 300. Globally branded companies employing staff from scores of different countries have budgets that are greater than those of individual countries. Images of the blue earth from space or the golden arches of McDonald's are ubiquitous across the world and especially upon the billion or so TV sets. A huge array of public and private organizations has arisen seeking to produce, govern, surveil, terrorize and entertain this 'spaceship earth', including some 17,000 trans-border civic associations.

Thus new technologies are producing 'global times' in which the distances between places and peoples again seem to be dramatically reducing. Some writers even suggest that time and space are 'de-materializing', as people, machines, images, information, power, money, ideas and dangers are all, we might say, 'on the move', travelling at bewildering speed in unexpected directions from place to place, from time to time.

Various commentators have tried to understand these exceptional changes. Anthony Giddens (1990) has described modern social life as being like a massive out-of-control 'juggernaut' lurching onwards but with no driver at the wheel. The journalist Frances Cairncross (1995) describes in detail the 'death of distance' that these various technologies seem to produce. Zygmunt Bauman (2000) talks of the speeded-up 'liquid modernity' as opposed to the fixed and given shapes that the modern world had earlier taken. Manuel Castells (2001) has elaborated the growth of an 'Internet galaxy' that has ushered the world into a wholly different informational structure. Michael Hardt and Antonio Negri (2000) have provocatively suggested that notions of nation-state sovereignty have been replaced by a single system of power, what they call 'empire', while many writers, indeed more than 100 a year, have described and elaborated the so-called globalization of economic, social and political life.

In this book I show how various 'global' processes raise major implications for most of the categories by which sociology and the other social sciences have examined the character of social life.

'Globalization' debates transform many existing sociological controversies, such as the relative significance of social structure, on the one hand, and human agency, on the other. Investigating the global also dissolves strong dichotomies between human subjects and physical objects, as well as that between the physical sciences and the social sciences. The study of the global disrupts many conventional debates and should not be viewed as merely an extra level or domain that can be 'added' to existing sociological analyses that can carry on regardless. 'Sociology' will not be able to sustain itself as a specific and coherent discourse focused upon the study of given, bounded or 'organized' capitalist societies. It is irreversibly changed.

So far, however, globalization studies are at an early stage of recording, mapping, classifying and monitoring the 'global' and its effects (see Castells 1996, 1997, 1998; Held et al. 1999; Scholte 2000). A new social science paradigm, of globalization, is developing and extending worldwide, but so far it remains somewhat 'pre-scientific'. It concentrates upon the nature of the global 'region' that is seen as competing with, and dominating, the societal or nation-state 'region'. Globalization studies pose a kind of inter-regional competition between the global and each society, the global on such a view being regarded as an overwhelming, singular causal force.

Whether writers are critics of, or enthusiasts for, the global, globalization gets attributed exceptional power to determine a massive range of outcomes. Furthermore, 'globalization' is often taken to refer both to certain processes (from the verb, to globalize) and to certain outcomes (from the noun, the globe). Both get designated as globalization, as both 'cause' and 'effect' (Rosenberg 2000).

In order to develop the analysis here I suggest there are five major globalization debates and claims that should be clearly distinguished from each other. There is no single and agreed-upon globalization thesis. These five theories are based respectively upon the concepts of structure, flow, ideology, performance and complexity. Each recurs at different points in this book – but I especially develop the implications of the last. This book sets out and defends a complexity approach to globalization, an approach that elaborates the *systemic* and *dynamic* character of what I previously called 'disorganized' capitalism.

The structural notion of the global

Chase-Dunn, Kawano, and Brewer (2000: 78) maintain that globalization is defined as the increased density of international and global interactions, compared with such interactions at the local or national levels (see Castells 1996; Held et al. 1999; Scholte 2000). There has been an increase in structural globalization with the greatly heightened density of such global interactions, although this is not simply a new phenomenon. This increased density of interactions is seen to result from a number of causes. There is the liberalization of world trade and the internationalizing of the organization of much capitalist production. There is the globalizing of the consumption of many commodities and the declining costs of transportation and communications. Inter-regional organizations are more significant with the internationalizing of investment and the general development of a 'world system'.

These together produce a revised structural relationship between the heightened density of the global *and* the relatively less networked, less dense, local/national levels. Globalization is not the property of individual actors or territorial units. It is an emergent feature of the capitalist economy as a whole, developing from the interconnections between different agents, especially through new forms of time–space 'distanciation' across the globe *and* of the compression of time–space relations (Jessop 2000: 356). This produces the 'ecological dominance' of globalizing capitalism.

Relatedly it is argued that this dominance both stems from, and reflects, the growth of a 'transnational capitalist class' that is centred within transnational corporations that are 'more or less in control of the processes of globalization' (Sklair 2001: 5). US presidential candidate Ralph Nader summarized this thesis through the concept of 'corporate globalization'.

The global as flows and mobilities

These flows are seen as moving along various global 'scapes', including the system of transportation of people by air, sea, rail, motorways and other roads. There is the transportation of objects via postal and other systems. Wire, coaxial and fibre-optic cables carry telephone messages, television pictures and computer information and images. There are microwave channels that are used for mobile phone communications. And there are satellites used for transmitting and receiving phone, radio and television signals (Appadurai 1990; Lash and Urry 1994; Castells 1996; Held et al. 1999). It is argued that, once such physical and organizational scape structures are established, then individuals, companies, places and even societies try to become nodes within such scapes.

Various potential flows occur along these scapes. Thus *people* travel along transportation scapes for work, education and holidays. *Objects* that are sent and received by companies and individuals move along postal and other freight systems. *Information, messages and images* flow along various cables and between satellites. *Messages* travel along microwave channels from one mobile phone to another.

These scapes and flows create new inequalities of access. What becomes significant is the 'relative', as opposed to the 'absolute', location of a particular social group or town or society in relationship to these multiple scapes. They pass by some areas while connecting others along information and transportation rich 'tunnels'. These can compress the distances of time and space between some places while enlarging those between others (Brunn and Leinbach 1991; Graham and Marvin 2001).

Globalization as ideology

This neo-liberal view is articulated by transnational corporations and their representatives and by various politicians and journalists (see Fukuyama 1992; Ohmae 1992). Such corporations operate on a worldwide basis and often lack any long-term commitment to particular places, labour forces or even societies. Thus those with economic interests in promoting capitalism across the globe maintain that globalization is both inevitable and natural *and* that national states or nationally organized trade unions should not regulate or direct the inevitable march of the global marketplace. What is viewed as crucial is 'shareholder value', so that labour markets should be made more flexible and capital should be able to invest or disinvest in industries or countries at will.

In this account, globalization is seen as forming a new epoch, a golden age of cosmopolitan 'borderlessness'. National states and societies are thought unable to control the global flows of information. Such a borderless world is seen as offering huge new opportunities to overcome the limitations and restrictions that societies and especially national states have historically exercised on the freedom of the 44,000 trans-border corporations to treat the world as 'their oyster'. There were incidentally only 7,000 such corporations in the 1960s (Scholte 2000: 86). The World Trade Organization both symbolizes this neo-liberal notion of globalization as ideology and represents such an interest, often spreading such notions through closed seminars for business leaders, academics and free-market politicians (see account and critique in Monbiot 2000).

Globalization as performance

Drawing on ideas about the analysis of gender as involving enactment, process and performance, Franklin et al. (2000: 1–17) argue that the global is not so much a 'cause' of other effects but an effect. It is enacted, as aspiration rather than achievement, as effect rather than condition, and as a project to be achieved rather than something that is pre-given. The global is seen as coming to constitute its own domains. It is continuously reconstituted through various material and semiotic processes. Law and Hetherington maintain that 'global space, is a material semiotic effect. It is something that is made' (1999).

And to perform the global implies that many individuals and organizations mobilize around and orchestrate phenomena that possess and demonstrate a global character. A good example of this involves how the idea of a separate and massively threatened 'global nature' has been produced and performed. What were once many apparently separate activities are now regarded as interconnected components of a single global crisis of the natural world (see Wynne 1994). This global nature has resulted from fusing various social practices that are remaking space. These include images of the earth from space and especially the Apollo 17 photograph of the 'whole earth' taken in 1972, transport policies, deforestation, energy use, media images of threatened iconic environments which are often markers of global threats, dramatic environmental protests, scientific papers on climate change, the ending of the cold war, NGO campaigns, records of extreme weather events, pronouncements by global public figures, global conferences such as Rio and Kyoto, and so on. Together these practices are performing a 'global nature', a nature that appears to be undergoing change that needs to be vigorously and systematically resisted and indeed reversed.

Global complexity

This conception is nowhere developed in detail, but Rifkin (2000: 191–3) analyses the implications of what he calls the 'new physics' for the study of property relations in the emerging capitalist world (see also Capra 2002). Rifkin notes that contemporary 'science' no longer sees anything 'as static, fixed and given'. The observer changes that which is observed, apparent hard-and-fast entities are always comprised of rapid movement, and there is no structure that is separate from process. In particular, time and space are not to be regarded as containers of phenomena, but rather all physical and social entities are constituted through time and through space. These ideas from the 'new physics' will be elaborated below, so as to explore better the extraordinary transformations of time–space that 'globalization' debates both signify and enhance.

Complexity does not, of course, solve all the problems of the social sciences. Nor is globalization only and exhaustively comprehensible through complexity. And most of all I am not suggesting that the 'social' implications of complexity are clear-cut. But I do suggest that, since the systemic features of globalization are not well understood, the complexity sciences may provide concepts and methods that begin to illuminate the global as a system or series of systems (for a similar formulation from within 'complexity', see Capra 2002).

In coupling together the 'global' and 'complexity', the aim is to show that the former comprises a set of emergent systems possessing properties and patterns that are often far from equilibrium. Complexity emphasizes that there are diverse networked time–space paths, that there are often massive disproportionalities between causes and effects, and that unpredictable and yet irreversible patterns seem to characterize all social and physical systems.

Some of this 'new physics' is also present in the so far most significant examination of the new global order, Manuel Castells's *The Information Age* (1996, 1997, 1998). His argument rests upon a 'complexity' conception of the global, although this is somewhat buried in the astonishing mass of material he presents. I now set out aspects of his argument, especially relating to the concept of 'network', before noting its 'complexity' components. His focus on networks will also be central to the analysis that follows below.

The Network Society

Castells (2000) argues that there are various technological paradigms, a cluster of interrelated technical, organizational and managerial innovations. Their advantages lie in their superior productivity in accomplishing assigned goals through synergy between their components. Each paradigm is constituted around a fundamental set of technologies, specific to the paradigm, and whose coming-together into a synergistic set establishes the paradigm.

Castells views information/communication technologies (including genetic engineering) as the basis of the new paradigm that developed within especially North America during the 1970s and 1980s. The main properties of this new informational paradigm are that the building blocks are bits of electronically transmitted information. Such technologies are pervasive, since information has become integral to almost all forms of human practice. Complex and temporally unpredictable patterns of informational development occur in a distributed fashion in very specific localities. Technologies are organized through loosely based and flexibly changing networks. These different technologies gradually converge into integrated informational systems, especially the once-separate biological and microelectronic technologies. Such systems permit organizations to work in real time 'on a planetary scale'. These instantaneous electronic impulses produce a 'timeless time' and provide material support for the development of new scapes, with the instantaneous flows of information being the precondition for the growth of global relations.

This new informational paradigm is characterized by the network enterprise (see Castells 1996, 2000, 2001). This is a network made from either firms or segments of firms, and/or from internal segmentation of firms. Large corporations are internally decentralized as networks. Small and medium businesses are connected in networks. These networks connect among themselves on specific business projects, and switch to another network when the project is finished. Major corporations work in a strategy of changing alliances and partnerships, specific to a given product, process, time and space. Furthermore, these cooperations are increasingly based on the sharing of information. These are information networks, which, in the limit, link up suppliers and customers through one firm, with this firm being essentially an intermediary of supply and demand. The unit of this production process is the business project.

What are important, therefore, are not 'structures', which imply a centre, a concentration of power, vertical hierarchy and a formal or informal constitution. Rather, networks 'constitute the new social morphology of our societies, and the diffusion of networking logic substantially modifies the operation and outcomes in processes of production, experience, power and culture . . . the network society, characterized by the pre-eminence of social morphology over social action' (Castells 1996: 469). A network is a set of interconnected nodes, the distance between social positions being shorter where such positions constitute nodes *within* a network as opposed to those lying outside that particular network. Networks are dynamic open structures so long as they continue to effect communication with new nodes (Castells 1996: 470–1; see also Castells 2000). Networks decentre performance and share decision making. What is in the network is useful and necessary for its existence.

What is not in the network will be either ignored if it is not relevant to the network's task, or eliminated if it is competing in goals or in performance. If a node in the network ceases to perform a useful function, it is phased out from the network, and the network rearranges itself. Some nodes are more important than others, but they all need each other as long as they remain within the network. Nodes increase their importance by absorbing more information and processing it more efficiently. If they decline in their performance, other nodes take over their tasks. Thus, the relevance and relative weight of nodes come not from their specific features, but from their ability to be trusted by the rest of the network. In this sense, the main nodes are not centres, but switchers that follow a networking logic rather than a command logic, in their function vis-à-vis the overall structure.

Networks generate complex and enduring connections stretching across time and space between peoples *and* things (Murdoch 1995: 745). Networks spread across time and space, which is advantageous, because 'left to their own devices *human actions and words do not spread very far at all*' (Law 1994: 24; see also Rycroft and Kash 1999). Different networks possess different abilities to bring home to certain nodes distant events, places or people, to overcome the friction of space within appropriate periods of time. According to Castells, there are now many very varied phenomena organized through networks, including network enterprises (such as the criminal economy), networked states (such as the European Union) and many networks within civil society (such as NGOs resisting globalization or international terrorists).

Castells's network analysis is of major importance, because it breaks with the idea that the global is a finished and completed totality. And he uses various ideas that prefigure a complexity approach to global phenomena (for a brief comment, see Castells 1996: 64–5). The analysis of networks emphasizes contingency, openness and unpredictability, suggesting analogies with how the 'web of life', according to Capra (1996: 35), consists of 'networks within networks'. Castells also emphasizes how networks of power produce networks of resistance. Many social practices are drawn to what could be called in complexity terms the 'power-resistance attractor' (Castells 1997: 362). He also argues that the strength of networks results from their self-organizing and often short-term character and not from centralized hierarchical direction, as with older style rational-legal bureaucracies of the sort famously examined by Weber (see Rycroft and Kash 1999; Rifkin 2000: 28). Specifically, Castells shows the 'chaotically' subversive effects of the development of the *personal* computer in the 1980s upon the workings of the *state* bureaucracy in the Soviet Union. This Weberian bureaucracy had historically controlled all information flows, including even access to the humble photocopier. But it was completely outflanked by the informational effects of the unpredictable global spread of the PC (Castells 1996: 36–7; 1998: ch. 1).

Castells also notes how attempts to regulate the Internet seem doomed to failure, since, as three American judges have written: 'Just as the strength of the Internet is chaos, so the strength of our liberty depends upon the chaos and cacophony of the unfettered speech the First Amendment protects' (Castells 1997: 259). The weakness of hierarchical nation states can be seen in the growth of the 'global criminal economy' and the exceptional mobility of illegal money and its transmutation (money laundering) as it careers around global scapes, often evading detection (Castells 1998: 201–3; this money movement being partly created by different nation-state regimes). This global criminal economy, or indeed global terrorism, takes the global order far from equilibrium, as nation states respond to such mobilities with attacks on civil liberties especially of mobile immigrant groups, and as global crime corrupts democratic politics in many societies. Castells (1998: 162) also talks of the 'black holes' of informational capitalism, places of time–space warping where peoples and places are drawn into a downwards and irreversible spiral or vortex from which there is no escape. He argues, similarly, as we will see, to Prigogine, that the global world is characterized not by a single time but by what he calls multiple times. There is clock time of the mass production factory, the timeless time of the computer and the glacial time of the environment (Castells 1996: ch. 7; 1997: 125; Urry 2000b: ch. 5).

However, Castells's *magnum opus* lacks a set of interrelated concepts that would enable these very diverse phenomena to be *systematically* understood. The global remains rather taken for granted and there is not the range of theoretical terms necessary to analyse the emergent properties of the networked 'global' level. In particular, the term 'network' is expected to do too much theoretical work in the argument. Almost all phenomena are seen through the single and undifferentiated prism of 'network'. This concept glosses over very different networked phenomena. They can range from hierarchical networks such as McDonald's to heterarchic extremely inchoate 'road protest movements', from spatially contiguous networks meeting every day to those organized around imagined 'cultures at a distance', from those based upon strong ties to those based on very important and extensive 'weak ties', and from those that are pretty well purely 'social' to those that are fundamentally 'materially' structured. These are all networks, but they are exceptionally different in their functioning one from the other.

Moreover, the concept of network does not bring out the enormously complex notions of power implicated in the diverse mobilities of global capitalism, such as those of the Internet (but see Castells 2001). Movement and power are now inextricably intertwined, and the concept of network minimizes the astonishing paradox, uncertainty and irreversibility of the patterns of global emergence. It is the materials, concepts and arguments within the science of complexity that remain undeveloped in Castells's otherwise brilliant examination of intersecting global networks.

The Challenge of Complexity

Thus, although hundreds of books and articles have been written on the 'global', it has been insufficiently theorized. In this book I turn to the complexity theory that is now emerging more generally as a potential new paradigm for the social sciences, having transformed much of the physical and biological sciences.

Thus 'non-linear' scientists working at one of the leading scientific complexity centres, the Santa Fe Institute in New Mexico, have developed some implications of complex adaptive systems for theorizing the nature of the global, especially the idea of global sustainability (Waldrop 1994: 348–53). Moreover, the US-based Gulbenkian Commission on the Restructuring of the Social Sciences, chaired by Immanuel Wallerstein and including non-linear scientist Ilya Prigogine, has advocated breaking down the division between 'natural' and 'social' science through seeing both domains as characterized by 'complexity' (Wallerstein 1996). Complexity, they say, involves not 'conceiving of humanity as mechanical, but rather instead conceiving of nature as active and creative', to make 'the laws of nature compatible with the idea of events, of novelty, and of creativity' (Wallerstein 1996: 61, 63). The Commission recommends how scientific analysis 'based on the dynamics of non-equilibria, with its emphasis on multiple futures, bifurcation and choice, historical dependence, and . . . intrinsic and inherent uncertainty', should be the model for the social sciences and this would undermine clear-cut divisions between humans and nature, and between social and natural science. However, most surprisingly this Commission is silent on the study of globalization, although the global is surely characterized by emergent and irreversible complexity and by processes that are simultaneously social *and* natural.

I show in various chapters how concepts and theories in chaos and complexity theory bear directly upon the nature of the global. In particular, complexity examines how components of a system can through their dynamic interaction 'spontaneously' develop collective properties or patterns, such as colour, that do not seem implicit, or at least not implicit in the same way, within individual components. Complexity investigates emergent properties, certain regularities of behaviour that somehow transcend the ingredients that make them up. Complexity argues against reductionism, against reducing the whole to the parts. And in so doing it transforms scientific understanding of far-from-equilibrium structures, of irreversible times and of non-Euclidean mobile spaces. It emphasizes how positive feedback loops can exacerbate initial stresses in the system and render it unable to absorb shocks to re-establish the original equilibrium. Positive feedback occurs when a change tendency is reinforced rather than dampened down. Very strong interactions occur between the parts of such systems, with the absence of a central hierarchical structure that unambiguously 'governs' and produces outcomes. These outcomes are to be seen as both uncertain *and* irreversible.

Another way of expressing this is to argue that complexity can illumine how social life is always a significant mixture of achievement *and* failure. Much social science is premised upon the successful achievement of an agent's or system's goals and objectives. Sociology is 'imbued with a commitment to and confidence in the possibility of increased success in social life'; the social world to which it directs our attention 'is one conceptualised, for the most part, in terms of practices, projects and processes that operate relatively unproblematically' (Malpas and Wickham 1995: 38). On this account, failure is 'an aberration, a temporary breakdown within the system', the exception rather than the rule (Malpas and Wickham 1995: 38). Thus there are the systems investigated by sociology (or the social sciences more generally) and there is failure or breakdown. There is thought to be either one or the other. It is a duality.

And yet, of course, social life is full of what we may term 'relative failure', both at the level of individual goals and especially at the level of social systems. Failure is a 'necessary consequence of incompleteness' and of the inability to establish and sustain complete control of the complex assemblages involved in any such system (Malpas and Wickham 1995: 39–40). This is well known but tends to be viewed in the social sciences through the concept of unintended consequences. What is intended is seen as having a range of unintended side effects that may take the system away from what seems to have been intended. However, this is a limited and often individualistic way of formulating relative failure that does not explicate just how these so-called side effects may be systemic features of the system in question. The use of complexity should enable us to break with such dualistic thinking, of system *and* its failures. Chaos and order are always interconnected within any such system.

It is in the light of these arguments that the emergent level of the global is examined below. Such a system clearly seems to combine in curious and unexpected ways, both chaos and order. It is not simply another region like that of society, nor is it the product of, or to be reduced to, a pre-existing difference or some governing element. Global systems can be viewed as interdependent, as self-organizing and as possessing emergent properties. I suggest that we can examine a range of non-linear, mobile and unpredictable 'global hybrids' always on the 'edge of chaos'. These should constitute the subject matter of sociology and of its 'theory' into the twenty-first century. Examples of such global hybrids include informational systems, automobility, global media, world money, the Internet, climate change, the oceans, health hazards, worldwide social protest and so on. Sociology has known that it deals with an open system. But the proliferation of inter-dependently fluid global hybrids operating at immensely varied time–space scales produces a quantum leap in the openness and complexity of the systems being analysed, systems always combining success and failure that are on the edge of chaos.

Moreover, although contemporary social-physical phenomena are undeniably networked, they should not be viewed merely as networks. Castells's notion of 'network society' does not capture the dynamic properties of global processes. 'Network' is too undifferentiated a term here. We need a significant battery of other terms to characterize the dynamic and emergent relationships between such networks, to develop the intense relationality of worldwide connections.

In particular, I examine how, given the range of possibilities that a system may move within, the trajectories of many systems are drawn over time to what complexity terms 'attractors'. The strange attractor of 'glocalization' is developed below, an attractor that involves parallel processes through which globalization-deepens-localization-deepens-globalization and so on. Both the global and the local are bound together through a dynamic, irreversible relationship, as huge flows of resources are drawn into and move backwards and forwards between the two. Neither the global nor the local can exist without the other. Diverse social and physical phenomena, including existing societies, are attracted towards the 'glocal', which develops in a symbiotic, irreversible and unstable set of relationships. I try to show that both the so-called global and local levels get transformed through billions of iterations that are irreversibly over time drawn towards, and are remade through, this glocalizing attractor.

Conclusion

Thus it is argued in this book that an appropriate analysis of the 'global age' necessitates the examination of various notions that are not reducible to, or explained through, single processes such as network or empire or markets or disorganization (Rescher 1998). Rather, global ordering is so immensely complicated that it cannot be 'known' through a single concept or set of processes.

Indeed, it is epistemologically and ontologically unknowable, with efforts at comprehension changing the very world that is being investigated. But, because of the power of metaphor in thinking, some notions from complexity will be interrogated in order to assess their fruitfulness in representing those processes implicated in such global ordering.

The book thus seeks to discuss how much complexity can illuminate an array of issues. First, are there *emergent* global systems? How is an emergent system of the 'global' developing that may be *self-producing* over time, such that its outputs provide inputs into a circular system of global objects, identities, institutions and social practices?

Second, what are the power and reach of such global systems? What is the impact of such systems upon the 'society system'?

Third, how are the properties of such systems reproduced through *iteration* over time involving 'inhuman' combinations of objects and social relations, or what I call 'material worlds'?

Fourth, how should we expect global 'systems' that are often far from equilibrium to develop and change irreversibly over time, especially in relationship to *small events* that can have big effects (and vice versa)?

Finally, what does 'global complexity' mean for the sociological problem of *social order* that has normally been seen as operating within and through individual 'societies'? How does a social ordering emerge through diverse and intersecting material worlds operating over varied times and moving across multiple spaces, where systems are always 'on the edge of chaos'? Can there any longer be societal ordering where cultures operate 'at a distance'?

This array of questions and issues provides the basis for what I have described and advocated elsewhere as 'mobile sociology' (Urry 2000a). The next chapter turns specifically to the challenge of a turn to complexity.

2

The Complexity Turn

Introduction

In this chapter some of the main characteristics of what has come to be known as the complexity sciences are elaborated. In this non-mathematical account, chaos theory, the non-linear and complexity are treated as a single paradigm. I thus artificially stabilize a set of sciences that are in fact open-ended, uncertain, evolving and self-organizing (see the 'complexity' account of 'complexity' in Thrift 1999).

I am not proposing a simple 'transfer' of complexity from the physical world into the social world. This is because complexity anyway analyses all phenomena that possess dynamic system properties, whether these are population of flies, firms or people. Indeed, significant work at the centrally important Santa Fe Institute concerned the implications of increasing returns for *economic* populations (Arthur 1994a; Waldrop 1994). Complexity is thus not simply a theory of the 'physical world' since it deals with the physics of all populations that demonstrate statistical probabilities whatever their apparent provenance (Prigogine 1997: 5, 35; hence the irrelevance of P. Stewart's critique (2001) of such a naturalist move).

Moreover, most significant phenomena that the so-called social sciences now deal with are in fact hybrids of physical *and* social relations, with no purified sets of the physical or the social. Such hybrids include health, technologies, the environment, the Internet, road traffic, extreme weather and so on. These hybrids, most of which are central in any analysis of global relations, are best examined through developing complexity analyses of the interdependent material–social, or 'inhuman' worlds. Through examining their dynamic interdependencies via complexity, their emergent properties can be effectively understood. The very division between the 'physical' and the 'social' is itself a socio-historical product and one that appears to be dissolving. The complexity sciences seem to provide the best means of transcending such outdated divisions, between nature *and* society, between the physical sciences *and* the social sciences (see Knorr-Cetina 1997; Macnaghten and Urry 1998).

This book attempts to transcend these divisions as well as those of determinism and free will, thus developing parallel claims to Capra's recent efforts (2002) to theorize the social world as complex living systems. It will do so by investigating the non-linear, statistical properties of various 'global systems' that often move unpredictably and yet irreversibly away from points of equilibrium. In complexity analyses there are presumed to be neither separate agents nor deterministic laws; there is a kind of in-betweenness that is neither deterministic nor involving free will.

Time and Space

Most of the social sciences presume that they deal with historical phenomena, while the physical world deals with ahistorical timeless phenomena. In this section I show how twentieth-century science transformed the understanding of time in the physical world. The physical and social sciences now appear to employ rather similar notions of historical time (Adam 1990). In *The Web of Life* Fritjof Capra argues that nature 'turns out to be more like human nature – unpredictable, sensitive to the surrounding world, influenced by small fluctuations' (1996: 187). This therefore suggests enormous interdependencies, parallels, overlaps and convergences between analyses of the physical *and* of the social worlds (Prigogine 1997; Capra 2002; and, from post-structuralism, Cilliers 1998; Rasch and Wolfe 2000). The absence of prediction does not invalidate a naturalist account of science (P. Stewart

2001: 328–9). Complexity authorizes 'scientific' accounts of the unpredictable but nevertheless strangely ordered.

Pre-twentieth-century science had operated with a view of time derived from Newton. He said of what he called absolute time, that, from 'its own nature, [it] flows equably without relation to anything eternal . . . the flowing of absolute time is not liable to change' (quoted in Adam 1990: 50). Such a view of absolute time is invariant, it is infinitely divisible into space-like units, it is measurable in length, it can be expressed as a number and it is reversible. It is time seen essentially as space, as a kind of Cartesian space comprising invariant measurable lengths that can be moved along, forwards *and* backwards as objects can move along the dimensions of space. Objects are viewed as contained within and strung out along the dimensions of absolute time and space.

The social sciences have historically insisted on the radical distinction between this natural time and what is often known as social time. However, most of what they have seen as specifically social time is now common throughout the understanding of the physical world (Adam 1990). What social science had treated as the specifically 'human' aspects of time seems now to characterize time within twentieth-century physical sciences.

Einstein showed that there is no fixed or absolute time independent of the system to which it refers. Time he saw as a local, internal feature of any system of observation and measurement. It varies on where and how it is measured. There is no objective absolute measurement of time. It can be stretched and shrunk. Further, Einstein demonstrated that time and space are not separate from each other but are fused into a four-dimensional time-space curved under the influence of mass (Coveney and Highfield 1990). Amongst various consequences are the possibility that the past could catch up with the future and especially the possibilities of time travel. In his *How to Build a Time Machine* Paul Davies (2001b) entertainingly describes the logical possibilities of travelling through time down what is called a 'wormhole'.

Time and space are thus not now viewed as the *container* of bodies that happen to move along the various dimensions (Casti 1994; Capra 1996; Prigogine 1997). The philosopher of science

A. N. Whitehead reflected on how *twentieth*-century physics would reject the notion that time and space stand *outside* the very relations between objects and subjects (D. Harvey 1996: 256–61). Time and space, he argues, are *internal* to the processes by which the physical and social worlds themselves operate, helping to constitute their very powers. Such a view leads to the thesis that there is not a single time but multiple times and that such times appear to flow. In the best-selling *A Brief History of Time*, Stephen Hawking summarizes how: 'Space and time are now dynamic qualities: when a body moves, or a force acts, it affects the curvature of space and time – and in turn the structure of space-time affects the way in which bodies move and forces act' (1988: 33).

Quantum theory generally describes a virtual state in which electrons appear to try out instantaneously all possible futures before settling into particular patterns. Quantum behaviour is instantaneous, simultaneous and unpredictable. The interactions between the parts are far more fundamental than the parts themselves. Bohm refers to this as the occurrence of a dance without dancers (see Zohar and Marshall 1994). Conventional notions of cause and effect do not apply within an indivisible whole where the interrelations between the parts are more fundamental than the individual parts. Really there are no parts at all as understood in mechanistic, reductionist thinking. There are only relationships, or, as Capra expresses it: 'the objects themselves are networks of relationships, embedded in larger networks . . . the relationships are primary' (1996: 37). Relationality is key here, a notion I will often return to.

Chrono-biology, or the biology of time, also shows not only that human societies experience time or organize their lives through time, but also that rhythmicity is a crucial principle of each organism and its relationships with its environment. Humans and other animals themselves appear to be 'clocks'. Plants and animals possess a system of time that regulates their functions on a twenty-four-hour cycle. Recent research has revealed timekeeping genes. Biological time is thus not confined to ageing but expresses the nature of biological beings as temporal, dynamic and cyclical. Change in living nature involves the notions of becoming and rhythmicity. Adam argues therefore that: 'Past, present, and future, historical time, the qualitative experience of time, the structuring of "undifferentiated change" into episodes, all are established as integral time aspects of the subject matter of the natural sciences' (1990: 150) and are by no means confined to the social world (see also Prigogine 1997).

More generally, thermodynamics shows that there is an irreversible flow of time. Rather than there being time symmetry and indeed a reversibility of time as postulated in classical physics, a clear distinction is drawn between the past and future. An arrow of time results within open systems in the loss of organization and an increase in randomness or disorder over time. This accumulation of disorder or positive entropy results from the Second Law of Thermodynamics (Coveney 2000).

However, there is not a simple growth of disorder. Prigogine shows how new order arises, but it is far from equilibrium. There are what he terms dissipative structures, islands of new order within a sea of disorder, maintaining or even increasing their order at the expense of greater overall entropy. He describes how such localized order 'floats in disorder' (cited in Capra 1996: 184). It is non-equilibrium situations that are sources of new order, as described below. For example, turbulent flows of water and air, which appear chaotic, are highly organized. Matter continuously flows into the vortex funnel of a whirlpool in a bath. The system is organizationally closed and maintains a stable form although it is far from equilibrium. Thus there is a paradoxical combination of continual flow and 'for-the-present' structural stability. In general, Prigogine and Stengers maintain in *Order out of Chaos* that it is the 'irreversibility [of time] . . . that brings order out of chaos' (1984: 292; see also Prigogine 1997: 164–73).

The most obvious illustration of this profound irreversibility of time is the expansion of the universe following the singular event of the 'big bang' fifteen billion or so years ago (Coveney and Highfield 1990). It is now thought that the universe began with such a 'big bang' without a pre-existing cause. The scientific discovery of the big bang cannot be reconciled with those laws of the physical world that see time as reversible, deterministic and involving 'classes of phenomena'. The big bang is a one-off phenomenon that is like nothing else ever to occur within the known universe. Laws of nature are thus to be treated as historical and not universal (Davies 2001a).

Moreover, the very phenomena of time and space are themselves historical. The big bang apparently created in that very moment both space and time. There was no pre-existing space and time: 'any attempt to explain the origin of the physical universe must perforce involve an explanation of how space and time came into existence too' (Davies 2001a: 57). There is therefore no 'time' before the big bang, and, if/when the universe ends in another singular event, time (and space) will also then cease. Space and time appear to have been spontaneously created, part of the systemic nature of the universe. They are suddenly switched on, through an unpredictable and yet apparently irreversible quantum change (Hawking 1988; Coveney and Highfield 1990; Casti 1994).

There are many mundane examples of irreversibility in the physical world: coffee always cools, organisms always age, spring follows winter and so on. There can be no going back, no re-absorbing of the heat, no return to youth, no spring before winter and so on. According to Eddington 'The great thing about time is that it goes on' (cited in Coveney and Highfield 1990: 83). The arrow or flow of time results in futures that are unstable, relatively unpredictable and characterized by various possibilities. Although time is irreversible, time is both multiple and unpredictable. Prigogine talks of the 'end of certainty' as the complexity sciences overcome what he calls the 'two alienating images of a deterministic world and an arbitrary world of pure chance' (1997: 189). Complexity thus repudiates the dichotomies of determinism and chance, as well as nature and society, being and becoming, stasis and change. Physical systems do not exhibit and sustain unchanging structural stability. The complexity sciences elaborate how there is order *and* disorder within all physical and social phenomena, including, according to Kauffman (1993), within evolution itself.

Systems are thus seen by complexity as being 'on the edge of chaos'. Order and chaos are in a kind of balance where the components are neither fully locked into place but yet do not fully dissolve into anarchy. Chaos is not complete anarchic randomness but there is a kind of 'orderly disorder' present within all such dynamic systems (see Hayles 1991, 1999).

Emergent Properties

A further consequence of this flowingness of time is that minor changes in the past are able to produce potentially massive effects in the present or future. Such small events are not 'forgotten'. Chaos theory in particular rejects the common-sense notion that only large changes in causes produce large changes in effects. Following a perfectly deterministic set of rules, unpredictable yet patterned results can be generated, with small causes on occasions producing large effects and vice versa. The classic example is the butterfly effect that was accidentally discovered by Lorenz in 1961. It was shown that miniscule changes at one location can theoretically produce, if modelled by three coupled non-linear equations, very large weather effects very far in time and/or space from the original site of the hypothetical wings flapping (Casti 1994: 96; Maasen and Weingart 2000: 93–4). Solutions to the equations in question are thus extremely sensitive to the specification of the initial conditions.

To express this point rather simply, there is no consistent relationship between the cause and the effect of some event. Rather, relationships between variables can be non-linear with abrupt switches occurring, so the same 'cause' can in specific circumstances produce quite different kinds of effect. Capra describes how much of the physical world is characterized by 'non-linearity': 'Nonlinear phenomena dominate much more of the inanimate world than we had thought, and they are an essential aspect of the network pattern of living systems' (1996: 122). Experiments on the population size of insect colonies show dramatic non-linear changes occurring through often small changes in birth rates and in the degree of overcrowding of that colony (see Casti 1994: 93–4). Over time the insect population dramatically rises and then falls with no movement towards any point of equilibrium.

Nevertheless there has been in Western societies a historical 'predisposition to kinds of explanation that posit a single central governor; that such explanations appear . . . more natural and conceptually simpler than global, interactive accounts' (Fox Keller

1985: 155). However, what in the end should convince are explanations that do capture this 'complexly interactive' nature of systems as a whole (Fox Keller 1985: 157). Complexity investigates the physics of such populations and their emergent, dynamic and self-organizing systemic properties (Prigogine 1997: 35). Such systems are unstable. A particular agent rarely produces a single and confined effect. Interventions or changes will tend to produce an array of possible effects right across the system in question (sometimes known as side effects). Prigogine describes these system effects as 'a world of irregular, chaotic motions' (1997: 155; see also, on 'system effects', Jervis 1997).

This notion of the non-linear or complexity involves three crucial presumptions. First, there is no necessary proportionality between 'causes' and 'effects' of events or phenomena. Second, there is no necessary equivalence between the individual and statistical levels of analysis. Thus what may characterize the individual will typically be very different from what is true at the statistical or system level. Third, the statistical or system effects are not the result of adding together the individual components. There is something else involved, normally known as emergence (Jervis 1997: ch. 2).

These points can be illustrated from the simple example of a pile of sand. If we consider such a pile and place an extra grain of sand on top, then the extra grain (the 'cause') either may stay there or it may cause a small avalanche. The system is self-organized without a 'central governor' and the effects of a particular local change can be enormously different (Cilliers 1998: 97). There is 'self-organized criticality' (Waldrop 1994: 304–6), with the pile of sand maintaining itself at the critical height. It is impossible to predict what the consequences will be of particular localized actions. The effects of the same 'cause' can be microscopic or global.

The central idea is that of 'emergence', that there are collective properties of all sorts of phenomena. Cohen and Stewart say that there are those 'regularities of behaviour that somehow seem to transcend their own ingredients' (1994: 232; see also Byrne 1998: ch. 3). It is not that the sum is greater than the size of its parts – but that there are system effects that are somehow different from its parts. Complexity examines how components of a system through their interaction 'spontaneously' develop collective properties or patterns, even simple properties such as colour, that do not seem implicit within, or at least not implicit in the same way, within individual components.

Thus the flavour of sugar is not present in the carbon, hydrogen and oxygen atoms that comprise it. The sublime taste of mayonnaise is so different from its mundane components (Capra 1996: 28; Cilliers 1998). The interdependent parts of a jumbo jet, through their very particular incredibly complex combination, produce the emergent property of enabling a 'plane' to fly. These are all striking non-linear consequences that are not present within, or reducible to, the very many individual components that comprise such activities (Jervis 1997).

Such large-scale patterns or properties emerge from, but are not reducible to, the micro-dynamics of the phenomenon in question. Thus gases are not uniform entities but comprise a seething confusion of atoms obeying the laws of quantum mechanics. The laws governing gases derive not from the behaviour of each individual atom but from their statistical patterning (Cohen and Stewart 1994: 232–3). The statistical pattern is different from and irreducible to the individual components. The key issue if that of relationality, a dance almost without dancers, according to Bohm.

Also, if a system passes a particular threshold with minor changes in the controlling variables, switches may occur and the emergent properties switch or turn over. Thus a liquid turns into a gas or relatively warm weather suddenly transforms into an ice age (Cohen and Stewart 1994: 21; Byrne 1998: 23). Leading non-linear scientist Nicolis summarizes how in a non-linear system: 'adding two elementary actions to one another can induce dramatic new effects reflecting the onset of cooperativity between the constituent elements. This can give rise to unexpected structures and events whose properties can be quite different from those of the underlying elementary laws' (1995: 1–2).

Moreover, there is the 'trap of linearity' (I. Stewart 1989: 83). So, although statisticians are aware of these complex and emergent properties, given the conventional 'repression of the non-linear', these normally get referred to and reduced to so-called interaction effects. But this is problematic, since, according to Byrne, 'complexity is locked away in the interaction term' (1998:

20). In order to elaborate such interaction effects and to unlock that complexity, further concepts are necessary, especially to separate out the different kinds of complex 'interconnections' characterizing physical and indeed social systems.

Attractors

In particular, the emergence of patterning within any given system stems from 'attractors'. If a dynamic system does not move over time through all possible parts of a potential or phase space but instead occupies a restricted part of it, then this is said to result from an attractor (Capra 1996: ch. 6). The simplest attractor is a point, as with the unforced swinging of a pendulum with friction. The simple system reaches the single point attractor. Metaphorically it can be said that 'the fixed point at the centre of the co-ordinate system "attracts" the trajectory' (Capra 1996: 130).

A somewhat more complex example is a domestic central heating/air conditioning system where the attractor consists, not of a single point, but of a specified range of temperatures. The relationship is not linear but involves what are called *negative* feedback mechanisms. These feedbacks minimize deviance and reestablish a specified range of temperatures. It is impossible to predict exactly what the precise temperature will be – only that it will lie within the range that constitutes the attractor. Topologically this attractor is like a doughnut, a system close to equilibrium in which effective negative feedback loops always bring the temperature back within the range specified within the system. This is a self-regulating and bounded system where negative feedback is crucial. Byrne suggests that this is analogous to social science studies of Fordism (see Byrne 1998: 28). An attractor and set of feedback mechanisms have for decades kept so-called Fordist societies within the range of possible alternatives within the doughnut ring and did not permit such societies to stray beyond the limits of the system in question.

In certain complex systems, though, there are 'strange attractors'. These are unstable spaces to which the trajectory of dynamical systems is attracted through billions of iterations. What are important here are *positive* feedbacks occurring over time that may take the system away from any point of equilibrium (Byrne 1998: 26–9). Either such a space may be indeterminate within the boundaries or there may be various sets of boundaries.

This dynamic instability can be seen in the butterfly-shaped Lorenz attractor (see its two-dimensional representation in Capra 1996: 133). Such attractors are immensely sensitive in the effects generated to slight variations in their initial conditions. Thus 'very small differences in the value of control parameters at the bifurcation point determine which of two radically different trajectories the system settles into' (Byrne 1998: 28). And, as iteration occurs time and time again, so an unstable and unpredictable patterned disorder develops that can be mathematically modelled. It is impossible to predict which point in such space the trajectory of an attractor will pass through, even though there are deterministic laws involved. Much recent science has been concerned to characterize the shaping or topology of such strange attractors. Iterations in non-linear systems result in values that topologically produce a kind of repeated stretching and folding effect, often known as the 'baker transformation' (Capra 1996: 132). These attractors presuppose complex mathematics and massive computerized calculations of the sort that has only been possible since the early 1970s.

Central to the patterning of attractors in time and space are the different kinds of feedback mechanisms. Early cybernetic research under the auspices of the Macy Conferences in the post-Second World War period emphasized the importance of negative feedback loops. These would have the effect of restoring the homeostatic functioning of whatever system was under examination. Such systems of circular causality involved the processing of information that resulted in the re-establishment of equilibrium and stability through negative feedback.

However, in later systems formulations, of complexity or the non-linear, positive feedback loops are examined. These are viewed as exacerbating initial stresses in the system, so rendering it unable to absorb shocks and re-establishing the original equilibrium (on the history of cybernetics, see Hayles 1999). Very strong interactions occur between the parts of a system and there is an absence of a central hierarchical structure able to 'govern' outcomes. Positive feedback occurs when a change tendency is reinforced rather than dampened down, as occurs with the negative feedback involved in a cybernetic central heating/air-conditioning system.

A social science application of positive feedback can be seen in the economic and sociological analyses of the increasing returns that can occur across a whole industry or activity. This can lay down irreversible path dependence where contingent events set into motion institutional patterns that have long-term deterministic properties (Mahoney 2000: 507). One example of this would be the way the privately owned 'steel-and-petroleum' car developed in the last decade of the nineteenth century and came to exert an awesome domination over other fuel alternatives, especially steam and electric power that were at the time preferable (Motavalli 2000). The 'path dependence' of the petroleum-based car was established and got 'locked' in.

Complexity theory generally analyses systems as unstable, dissipative structures. They are thermodynamically open and capable of assimilating large quantities of energy from the environment and simultaneously converting it into increased structural complexity (Reed and Harvey 1992: 360–2). Such systems also dissipate into their environment high levels of residual heat.

Such dissipative systems reach points of *bifurcation* when their behaviour and future pathways become unpredictable and new higher order, more differentiated, structures may emerge. Dissipative structures involve non-linearity, a flowingness of time, no separation of systems and their environment, and a capacity for the autopoeitic re-emergence of a new ordering far from any system equilibrium (Capra 1996: 89, 187). Systems appear to have the capability of reordering themselves into ever more complex structures following points of bifurcation.

Maturana and Varela famously developed the notion that any such systems are self-making or autopoietic (Maturana 1981; Mingers 1995). Such autopoiesis involves the idea that living systems entail a process of self-making or self-producing. Autopoiesis involves a network of production processes in which the function of each component is to participate in the production or transformation of other components in the network. In this way the network comes to make itself. It is produced by the components and these in turn produce the components. In a living system the product of its operation is its own organization, with the development of boundaries specifying the domain of its operations and defining the self-making system as such (Capra 1996: 98; Hayles 1999: ch. 6).

Autopoiesis can be seen in non-linear laser theory where the coordination of the required emissions is seen as carried out by the laser light itself through ongoing processes of self-organization (Capra 1996: 91–2). It can also be seen in the nature of urban growth. Small local preferences mildly expressed in the concerns of individuals, such as wanting to live with those who are ethnically similar, can lead to massively segregated neighbourhoods such as those characteristic of large American cities. Krugman argues that residential patterns are unstable in the face of random perturbations: 'local, short-range interactions can create large-scale [self-organizing] structure' (1996: 17). More generally, in the social sciences Luhmann has most elaborated the implications of autopoiesis for examining the long-term functioning of social systems.

Thus far I have set out some of the key notions in the sciences of complexity. I have briefly outlined the following concepts necessary for analysing the physical and social worlds: multiple times and spaces; the unpredictability and irreversibility of time; order and chaos; non-linear effects; emergence; bifurcation; negative and positive feedback; self-organization; and various attractors. In the rest of this chapter some important uses of complexity found in analyses that interrogate certain material worlds will be examined. In subsequent chapters elements of complexity will be connected to the very influential global debates now creating 'chaos' across many social sciences.

Complex Systems

We might begin by noting that there is an emerging 'structure of feeling' that complexity both signifies and enhances (Williams 1973; Thrift 1999). Such an emergent structure involves a greater sense of contingent openness available to people, corporations and societies, of the diversity of geographies, of a charity towards objects and nature, of the diverse and variegated patterning of relationships, households and persons, and of the sheer increase in the hyper-complexity of products, technologies and socialities (Rycroft and Kash 1999: 55; Thrift 1999: 53–9; Duffield 2001).

Complexity has already had a significant impact upon a huge range of social and intellectual discourses and practices, including alternative healing, architecture, consultancy, consumer design, economics, defence studies, fiction, garden design, geography, history, literary theory, management education, New Age, organizational learning, philosophy, post-structuralism, sociology, stock-car racing, town planning and so on. Notions of chaos and complexity move in unpredictable ways from discourse to discourse, practice to practice, creating on occasions a sense of a 'chaos cult' (Maasen and Weingart 2000: 125).

However, while most of the non-physical sciences have 'gone global' in the past decade, the major sociological applications of complexity remain strangely 'societal' (see Luhmann 1990, 1995; Reed and Harvey 1992; Baker 1993; Francis 1993; Mingers 1995; Keil and Elliott 1996; Eve et al. 1997; Biggs 1998; Byrne 1998; Cilliers 1998; Hayles 1999; Rycroft and Kash 1999; Medd 2000; Capra 2002).

And yet this is paradoxical, since 'complexity' practices can themselves be conceptualized as a self-organizing global network. Chaos/non-linear/complexity researchers deploy the techniques of PR and branding, international meetings, guru worship, networking especially centred on certain nodes such as Santa Fe or the various Research Institutes named after Prigogine, and the extensive use of global media (Waldrop 1994; Thrift 1999; Maasen and Weingart 2000).

We can begin here by noting how Robert Rycroft and Don Kash in *The Complexity Challenge* (1999: ch. 4) examine the complexity of the material worlds that are involved in various technological systems. They note that there has been a huge increase in the sheer number of components within products. The Eli Whitney musket of around 1800 had fifty-one components, while the space shuttle of the late twentieth century contained ten million. Second, there is the massive increase in the cybernetic contribution performed by architectures that integrate components through feedback loops, both in products such as cars, and in the process side of technology. The authors conclude that 'it is now normal for both product and process innovation to emphasize adjustment and adaptation through continuous feedback' (Rycroft and Kash 1999: 55). Such systems thus increasingly involve hardware, software and 'socialware'. Products and processes constitute systems that cannot be understood without social organizational features. Thus there are increasingly complex socio-technical systems or what I term material worlds.

Rycroft and Kash examine how there has been a huge shift towards complexity in contemporary economies. Even in 1970 the most valuable products in world trade were still simple products produced by simple processes, such as clothes, paper, yarn, meat, coffee and so on. But a mere quarter of a century later, only 14 per cent of the most valuable items in world trade are such simple products produced by simple processes. By 1995 nearly two-thirds of the most valuable products in world trade involved complex processes *and* complex products, involving vast numbers of components, cybernetic architectures and socio-technical systems (Rycroft and Kash 1999: 56–7).

This 'increasing complexity of products and processes with the greatest export value . . . is linked with self-organizing networks. Such network organizational systems are continuously self-reproducing themselves by developing the most sophisticated skills and structures necessary to innovate technologies that overcome obstacles, or create new pathways' (Rycroft and Kash 1999: 61–2). They go on to connect such self-reproduction to the importance of positive feedback and organizational learning within socio-technical systems or networks.

But if the history of recent technology shows the impossibility of conceiving of 'technologies' as merely non-human, so Stephen Budiansky's *Nature's Keepers* (1995) develops an excoriating critique of preserving apparently eternal and wild 'non-human' nature. 'Strict preservation through a hands-off or "natural" management policy has destroyed many of the very things that nature lovers claim to value the most' (Budiansky 1995: 8). Thus there is no such thing as 'nature's balance', no real or primordial nature that would be in equilibrium if only humans had not intruded. It is shown how the effects of humans are subtly and irreversibly woven into the very evolution of landscape. Countless forms of human habitation have affected all such systems over the millennia, especially the extensive and regular use of fire by original dwellers to clear land for primitive agriculture (as with native Americans in the USA). And any ecological system is immensely complex so that there are never straightforward policies that simply restore nature's balance. Ecological systems are always on the edge of chaos without a 'natural' tendency towards equilibrium, even if all humans were to depart forever from the earth (Budiansky 1995: 11).

Indeed many ecological systems themselves depend not upon stable relationships but upon massive intrusions, of extraordinary flows of species from other parts of the globe and of fire, lightning, hurricanes, high winds, ice storms, flash floods, frosts, earthquakes and so on. The '"normal" state of nature is not one of balance and repose; the "normal" state is to be recovering from the last disaster' (Budiansky 1995: 71). And it is such disasters, a swirling pattern of constant change, that produces the rich diversity of niches where micro-habitats can develop, although often these developments can only be seen over very lengthy periods of time. These periods are often much longer than the lives of particular researchers or of research programmes. It is therefore instability and change that makes for diversity and not a stable unchanging 'nature' in some supposed state of equilibrium. So, as Prigogine began to show in the 1960s, systems can be ordered but far from equilibrium.

Moreover, the population size of a species shows no tendency to stability, and especially not to rise smoothly to the presumed carrying capacity of its environment and then to level off and remain stable. Rather populations of most species demonstrate extreme unevenness, with populations often rising rapidly when introduced into an area and then almost as rapidly collapsing (Jervis 1997: 28). The food consumption of animal species responds in a non-linear and time-lagged fashion to changing circumstances and this produces massive unevenness of population size with no natural or equilibrium size (see Budiansky 1995: 90–5). Indeed, the chaotic properties of biological systems also make predictions of what favours the protection of a particular species pretty well impossible. Most interventions designed to protect some particular species actually triggered unforeseen side effects that made the species weaker than it had initially been (Budiansky 1995: 160–1).

This stunning unpredictability of the material world can also be seen from how even roadside and urban environments have become sites in which rapidly expanding and apparently irreversible populations of various animal and plant species have dramatically emerged. These are sites that are well away from what would appear to be the 'natural' habitats of such species. The 'urban' and the 'wild' are no longer exclusive categories (Budiansky 1995; Clark 2000; Davis 2000a). Thus rats and foxes are plentiful within European cities, while, around Los Angeles, coyotes, skunks, squirrels, rats, killer bees, wild dogs, racoons and even mountain lions are rapidly increasing in numbers as they switch from specific predation to a broader-based opportunistic feeding – in the case of lions, now feeding on small rodents, pets, human garbage and increasingly humans (on 'non-linear lions', see Davis 2000a: 249).

Through a non-linear reading of the turbulent 'city', Clark argues that 'in the very heartland of the social . . . there is a resurgence of "nature", and efflorescence of "life"' (2000: 29). There is a material world emerging in cities that is mobile, volatile and we might say cosmopolitan. There is no silent, docile 'nature', especially when confronted by new forms of 'culture'. Indeed, there are various emergent highly adaptable viruses, such as Aids and ebola, new superbugs, newly lethal pathogens such as prions, and the reappearance of TB, cholera and the bubonic plague. Such a medicalized 'apocalypse now' stems from novel patterns of global travel and trade, the heightened ineffectiveness of antibiotics that encounter increased 'resistance', and the development of new powerful risk cultures beyond and especially within 'medicine' itself (Van Loon 2002: ch. 6). This echoes De Landa's more general analysis of cities. He conceives of them as complex, dynamic and open systems containing exceptional flows and mixtures of the organic and the inorganic, the living and the non-living, the human and the non-human, culture and nature, the risky and the risk free (De Landa 1997; Clark 2000).

Mike Davis's *Ecology of Fear* examines one such city in detail. He concentrates upon some of the emergent material–social interchanges occurring in and around the paradigm twenty-first century city, Los Angeles (Davis 2000a: ch. 1). What was once thought of as the Land of Sunshine is being reinvented as the Apocalypse Theme Park. Between 1992 and 1995 in Los Angeles, floods were followed by riots, by floods, by firestorms, by a tornado, by an earthquake and by floods again. Nearly two million people were affected by disaster-related death, injury or damage to home and business. Half a million people left the city within two years. Southern California is characterized by the catastrophic coincidence of extreme events.

Moreover, this is not a random disorder but a dynamic pattern of escalating feedback loops resulting from the pattern of urban sprawl. Conditions that have produced this include the widespread growth of what has been called 'sloping suburbia', the overwhelming use of the automobile, the lack of public space, the concreting of the river basin, the building of houses in ecologically unsuitable areas, as well as global warming more generally. Extreme events, especially extreme weather events, demonstrate, according to Davis, 'the principle of nonlinearity where small changes in driving variables or inputs – magnified by feedback – can produce disproportionate, or even discontinuous, outcomes' (2000a: 19).

Malibu, the wildfire capital of North America, is particularly illustrative here (Davis 2000a: ch. 3). Various interdependent causes historically produce a particular intensity of fires in this area. What seems most significant is the non-linear relationship between the age structure of vegetation and the intensity of fires that are generated. Fifty-year-old trees burn fifty times more intensely than twenty-year-old trees. However, because of the highly influential residents living in the Malibu region, there has been since 1919 a policy of 'total fire suppression'. This has the effect that the smaller fires that are beneficial in recycling nutrients do not take place, and more importantly the bulk of trees in the area are much older and more intense in the fires that they subsequently produce. So the limitation on small fires results in greater and larger fires subsequently. And, further, the extreme fires that are intermittently generated transform the chemical structure of the soil, turning it into a water-repellent layer that dramatically accelerates subsequent sheet flooding and erosion (Davis 2000a: 100–3). Extreme fire events and massive flooding follow in a non-linear way from the intervention to prevent those limited fires that would otherwise constitute a routine feature of the Malibu ecosystem in Los Angeles.

This example shows that certain kinds of cause can generate huge and unpredictable change while other examples would show that external causes could generate almost no significant effects. There is, therefore, a lack of proportionality between 'causes' and 'effects', although we should bear in mind that there are really no such things as causes that are 'external' to such a system.

The character of such systems is specifically explored in Charles Perrow's *Normal Accidents*. He argues that, given certain system characteristics, multiple, unexpected and interacting failures are systemically inevitable (Perrow 1999: 5; see also Jervis 1997). Such accidents will occur when the system is tightly coupled, so that processes happen very fast and cannot be turned off, when the failed parts cannot be isolated and when there is no other way to keep the system going. With such tightly coupled systems, recovery from the initial disturbance that may have been relatively trivial is impossible. The consequences will spread quickly, chaotically and irreversibly throughout the system, so producing 'system accidents' rather than accidents caused by individual error (Perrow 1999: 11).

In loosely coupled systems by contrast there is plenty of slack in terms of time, resources and organizational capacity. They are much less likely to produce normal accidents since incidents can be coped with, so avoiding the interactive complexity found within the tightly coupled system. In the latter, moreover, the effects are non-linear. Up to a point, tightening the connections between elements in the system will increase efficiency when everything works smoothly. But, if one small item goes wrong, then that can have a catastrophic knock-on effect throughout the system. The system literally switches over, from smooth functioning to interactively complex disaster. And sometimes this results from a supposed improvement in the system. Thus improved safety within a car through the legally enforced wearing of seatbelts, or the enhanced safety systems on the *Titanic*, or the safety systems in railway signalling, can, in very particular conditions, produce correspondingly more dangerous behaviour and an increased likelihood of 'normal accidents' (Adams 1995; Jervis

1997: 68–9). What we might call the Titanic effect is a good example of the 'complex interconnectedness' of systems (on complexity theory, see Perrow 1999: 386). As Law maintains, on the basis of research on train crashes, 'system perfection is not only impossible but, more strongly, it may be *self defeating*' (2000: 14). On occasions, system fluidities or imperfections are essential for 'safety' because of the complex characteristics of the system in question.

There are some parallels between issues of system safety and the curious kinds of cooperation found between American stock-car drivers travelling at up to 190 m.p.h. on super-speedways (Ronfeldt 2001). These racers both cooperate *and* compete according to complex and emergent sets of rules. The drivers self-organize into cooperative draft lines and then intermittently form competitive break-out lines. They use radio communications to generate information and especially to seek out allies. According to Ronfeldt, 'this creates a fast-moving, dynamic structure, or system, that exhibits a kind of order – oscillating lines in front of a milling pack, tightly coupled and fraught with nonlinear processes – that is often on the verge of criticality, chaos and catastrophe' (2001: 17). Such stock-car racing could be seen as emblematic of US society. It involves peculiar combinations of cooperation and competition and results in complex system outcomes.

More generally, Manuel De Landa's *A Thousand Years of Nonlinear History* (1997) examines through the prism of complexity different kinds of systemic organization, especially of 'meshworks' (or networks of networks) and of hierarchy. He is especially concerned with the organization and consequences of the flows of various materials, especially of energy, genes and languages. Where such flows were dominated by 'hierarchical' homogenization (or tight coupling), as occurred through centuries of Chinese history, then explosive, self-organizing urban development did not take place. It is only with meshworks and a resulting 'freedom of motion' and 'maximum mobility' that a 'dynamic pattern of turbulent urban evolution in the West' occurs, involving intense and productive flows of energy, transportation and money (Braudel 1973: 396–7; De Landa 1997: 34–45). Cities are sites of interchange between various intersecting flows – and some cities develop the capacity for self–organization and massive growth.

Later I argue that it is only with such mobilities that complex systems develop in the 'social' world – through combinations of mobility and moorings.

More generally, De Landa develops a wide-ranging analysis of bodies, selves, cities and societies. He views these as merely 'transitory hardenings' in the more basic flows of minerals, genes, diseases, energy, information, and language that over the past millennium have swept across the earth's crust (De Landa 1997: 259–60). In examining 'global complexity', similar analyses are developed of the flows of such intersecting and non-linear 'material worlds' that intermittently realize 'transitory hardenings'.

Conclusion

Thus a wide array of complexity formulations has been introduced here; and a number of illustrative studies drawn on to suggest the usefulness of these approaches beyond the physical and biological sciences.

Such complexity analyses also emphasize that scientific observations are themselves components of the systems being investigated. There is nothing outside the system. Hence the notions of complex systems undermine certain 'realist' formulations that speak of an 'external world'. As Heisenberg expresses it: 'What we observe is not nature itself, but nature exposed to our method of questioning' (cited in Capra 1996: 40). This connectedness of science with its system of investigation has two major implications for what follows.

First, we need to ask if the particular physical and/or social system presents itself to the current practices of social science in ways that mean it can be systematically observed and analysed. What are the conditions of possibility of a science of that system or systems in question? What forms could it take given the current observational, measurement and theoretical practices of contemporary science? Second, we should ask if these practices of investigation themselves produce complex effects upon the system in question, in cases resulting in a self-fulfilling prophecy where research findings help to bring about the very effects that they are themselves investigating.

Both these points are pertinent to global systems. First, the enormously open character of global systems might mean that they are currently beyond systematic analysis. One could hypothesize that current phenomena have outrun the capacity of the social sciences to investigate. We should ask whether the global is constituted as a fit object of (social) science investigation. Are the observational, measurement and theoretical resources up to investigating the enormously complex character of global systems? My proposal here is that social science needs all the help that it can get to analyse such systems. This explains the necessity to turn to some of the theoretical resources of complexity that are centrally concerned with the processes of large-scale emergence. It seems reasonable to consider how and in what ways such complexity notions may pertain to examining the many processes of global emergence.

Second, the proliferation of huge numbers of 'global' analyses has in a way become part of the very system being investigated. They are helping to perform the global in part in a self-fulfilling manner. One element then of what needs investigation are the multiple ways in which across various systems the global comes to be performed through arguments, images, books, TV programmes, symposia, magazines and information that increasingly represent, speak and perform 'the global' (see Franklin et al. 2000).

In the next chapter I consider certain of these analyses of the global. I show that most are as yet insufficiently 'complex', while in subsequent chapters I develop the notion of 'global complexity', as the complexity turn in the social sciences is explored and hopefully enhanced.

3

Limits of 'Global' Analyses

Introduction

In this chapter I show the limitations of many globalization analyses that deal insufficiently with the *complex* character of emergent global relations. This is on the face of it surprising, because the paradigm of globalization would seem to connect to complexity ways of thinking, even where the language and techniques of complexity are not explicitly deployed.

Self-evidently, the analysis of globalization emphasizes that events happening in one place importantly impact upon many other places, often remote in time and in space (for details, see Goerner 1994). Giddens defined globalization as early as 1990: 'the intensification of worldwide social relations which link distant localities in such a way that local happenings are shaped by events occurring many miles away and vice versa' (1990: 64). The analysis of globalization brings out the obvious interdependencies between peoples, places, organizations and technological systems stretching across the world. These interdependencies involve economic, social, political and military happenings. With the analysis of globalization no place 'is an island'.

Complexity-researcher Chris Langton further maintained that: 'From the interaction of the individual components . . . emerges some kind of property . . . something you couldn't have predicted from what you know of the component parts. . . . And the global property, this emergent behaviour feeds back to influence the behaviour . . . of the individuals that produced it' (cited Thrift 1999: 33–4; see also Waldrop 1994: 329). Globalization analyses should bring out these global emergent properties, such as the fortunes of the world economy or global environmental change or cultural homogenization through the global media or the world-wide spread of representative democracies (see Held et al. 1999).

Within sociology the analysis of such global properties seems to 'solve' the debate between those advocating studying the social whole (methodological holists) and those advocating the explanation of social phenomena through accounts that begin with the individual (methodological individualists). There appears to be a new level of the social whole, the global, with emergent properties that are clearly not those of individuals, nor could be reduced in any sense to individuals. The study of the global level would appear to solve the problem of the relationship between structure and agency, with the former 'winning' the argument.

However, this book is premised upon the idea that many globalization analyses treat the emergent global properties as too unified and as too powerful. Their analysis is simplified, static and reductionist. This can be seen in formulations that state that 'globalization' is x or alternatively that 'globalization' does x. The advocates of, and the critics of, globalization 'assume a too linear trajectory of globalization and . . . make the paper tiger of globalization into a nasty and invincible bogeyman' (R. Keil 1998: 619). 'Globalization' I suggest is neither unified nor can act as a subject nor should it be conceived of in linear fashion.

Regions, Networks and Fluids

Thus I examine the idea of the global in terms of the distinctions between 'regions, networks and fluids' made by Annemarie Mol and John Law (1994; see also Urry 2000b). These distinctions are drawn on to bring out the varied spatial patterns or topologies that characterize diverse 'global' systems. What do these terms mean?

First, there are *regions* in which objects are clustered together. Regions are defined in terms of three orthogonal coordinates that specify each such cluster. Such a topology is familiar and regularly used in analysing each 'society'. Normally each society is deemed to be a region with clear and distinct boundaries drawn around each one.

Second, there are *networks* that stretch across diverse regions. Within a network as understood here there is a relational constancy between its components. These components deliver an invariant outcome, sometimes known as 'immutable mobiles', through the entire network crossing regional boundaries. Many scientific communities deliver such immutable mobiles across much of the network.

Third, there are *fluids* where 'neither boundaries nor relations mark the difference between one place and another. Instead, sometimes boundaries come and go, allow leakage or disappear altogether, while relations transform themselves without fracture. Sometimes, then, social space behaves like a fluid' (Mol and Law 1994: 643). Such fluids slowly transmutate as they move within and across space.

Thus there are three distinct spatial patterns, region, network and fluid, and the social sciences have failed to distinguish between them satisfactorily. In particular the idea of a fluid is perhaps the least familiar. Mol and Law use this notion to describe how anaemia is dealt with across the world. Mol and Law especially show the apparent differences between the treatments of anaemia in the Netherlands compared with various 'African' countries. They argue that there is no simple *regional* difference between its monitoring and treatment in the Netherlands compared with Africa. Nor though is there a single clinical *network* operating worldwide with elements that hang together through invariant relations that transport the same 'anaemia' to both the Netherlands and to 'Africa'. Rather than either region or network, they argue that: 'We're looking at *variation without boundaries and transformation without discontinuity*. We're looking at flows. The space with which we are dealing is *fluid*' (Mol and Law 1994: 658; emphasis in original).

'Anaemia', like blood, can be seen as a fluid, flowing in and out of different regions, across different borders, using diverse networks. It changes as it goes, although this is often in ways that are more or less imperceptible at the time. Anaemia as an illness is fluid-like, similar to blood, and subject to many transformations even as it remains as 'anaemia'. Fluids are subject to mixtures and

gradients with no necessarily clear boundaries. The objects generated may not be clearly defined. Normality is a gradient and not
a clear absolute. In a fluid space it is not possible to determine
identities once and for all. Various other fluids may combine
together with each other; thus a 'fluid world is a world of *mixtures*' (Mol and Law 1994: 660). Fluids are not solid or stable.
Moreover, fluids get around absences such as the location of a
laboratory in an African war zone and are contingent. In short,
Mol and Law (1994: 664) conclude:

> The study of fluids, then, will be a study of the relations, repulsions
> and attractions which form a flow. . . . So *how* does anaemia flow?
> How does it move between the Netherlands and Africa and back
> again? . . . It may flow in people's skills, or as part of the attribute
> of devices, or in the form of written words. . . . And as it moves, it
> changes its shape and character.

Mol and Law thus bring out the power of the fluid to account for
the uneven and heterogeneous skills, technologies, interventions
and tacit knowledge of those that are involved in monitoring and
treating anaemia in various clinics across the world. The extent
and power of such fluids stretching within and especially across
societal borders raise important questions about the power of
societies (as 'regions') to implement appropriate medical treatment or functioning economies. Especially the fluid of 'anaemia'
will take different forms as it gorges within, or trickles through,
any particular region. Such a fluid can be distinguished in terms
of the *rate* of flow, its *viscosity*, its *depth*, its *consistency* and its
degree of confinement within certain channels. The idea of a fluid
is a very important notion here that provocatively captures aspects
of how to think the global that the ideas of region and network
ignore. In the following I show how these distinctions of region,
network and fluid relate to societies and the study of the global.

Global Regions, Networks and Flows

I have shown elsewhere that social scientific work depends upon
metaphors and much theoretical debate consists of contestation

between different metaphors (see Urry 2000b: ch. 2). In particular, the sociological concept of society is organized around the metaphor of a *region* – namely, that 'objects are clustered together and boundaries are drawn around each particular cluster' (Mol and Law 1994: 643). There seem to be many different societies, each with its specific clustering of social institutions organized through a nation state, and with a clear and policed border surrounding each society *qua* region. Society qua bounded region has been central to notions of the nation state, democracy and citizenship for the past century or so.

One approach then to the study of globalization is also to view the global as a region involved in increasing inter-regional competition with each 'society'. In the 'struggle' between these two regions, many analysts presume that the global is winning, albeit in complicated ways, vis-à-vis each nation-state society. This is what has been called the hyperglobalist position (see Held et al. 1999: 3–7). For example, Martin and Schumann uncompromisingly write that globalization, 'understood as the unfettering of world-market forces and the removal of economic power from the state, is for most nations a brute fact from which they cannot escape' (1997: 216). And, according to Ohmae (1992), there is already a borderless world of global relations with the regions of 'society' across the world being wholly in retreat (see also Fukuyama 1992; Albrow 1996). The constraints of space or geography have been eliminated because of denationalized flows of information. This victory of the borderless global region is highly desirable for Ohmae.

Castells characterizes the contemporary world not as borderless, but nevertheless poised between 'the new, informational economy working on a global scale' (1996: 97) and 'the persistence of nations and national governments, and . . . the role of governments in using economic competition as a tool of political strategy' (1996: 99). There are thus two regions and an implacable competition between the two. Many writers of course treat the USA as central to global relations and hence see a regional conflict between the American hegemon, on the one hand, and individual nation states, whether in Europe, Asia or elsewhere, on the other (Chase-Dunn et al. 2000).

There are other writers who also see a war of the regions, but in this case where the region of the nation state is partly capable of winning vis-à-vis the region of the global. Hirst and Thompson (1996) particularly articulate this 'global sceptic' position. They maintain that the institutions of the nation state and especially of state institutions do possess 'causal efficacy' vis-à-vis the global (see also Mann 1997: 474).

However, these are limited ways of understanding the relationship between the global and societies because they all take the global to be in some ways a 'region'. In the rest of this chapter some deficiencies are outlined. First, viewing the global as a region involves the thesis of a 'territorial trap' (Brenner 1997). This involves 'a-historical state-centrism' in which the 'national and the global scales are viewed as being mutually exclusive rather than relational and co-constitutive' (Brenner 1997: 138). In the accounts I am criticizing, the global and the national are set apart from each other and then seen as involved in intense inter-regional competition. This can be seen when Robertson talks of 'the world-as-a-single-place', of an unambiguous global region (cited in Franklin et al. 2000: 3). Brenner argues rather that we should examine the complex sets of social relations *between* the national and the global. They constitute each other. In chapter 5 below the mathematics of a 'strange attractor' is used to demonstrate how the global and the national can be seen as co-constituting each other.

This issue can also be seen in those analyses of each national sovereign society, such as Hirst and Thompson's account (1996) of how certain regions of 'national economies and societies' can resist the spread of 'globalization'. And, analogously, in arguments of the 'hyperglobalists' such as Ohmae (1992), it is the global region that is overly unified and in equilibrium (see also Held et al. 1999). Both accounts imply both a societal or global totalization and *equilibrium*. The global functions both as 'process' and as 'outcome', as both 'cause' and 'effect'. There is a related failure to distinguish between a 'theory of globalization' (in terms of analysing a complex but incomplete set of determinants) and 'globalization theory' (where the global level appears to account for and to describe almost everything). Indeed, globalization does not itself explain anything very much, it has been said (on the 'follies of globalization theory', see Rosenberg 2000).

Also implicit in some of these 'regional' formulations is that space and time are treated as relatively static 'containers' of economic, social and political entities (Brenner 1997: 140). But in the previous chapter it was shown that complexity emphasizes how time and space flow and are productive. They are not simply containers or dimensions of 'objects', whether social or physical. The notion of competition between the 'societal' and the 'global' regions does not do justice to the complex, overlapping and evolving relations between diverse processes, including the ways in which societies do not necessarily possess properties that are also emergent at the global level.

Nor do such regional notions acknowledge that the 'global' level is in fact made up of very many 'polities', not just of the nation state and the global with a 'head-to-head' competition between them (see Walby forthcoming). There are also regional blocs (NAFTA, EU), globally organized religions (Islam, Catholic Church), international organizations (UN), international NGOs (Greenpeace) and international treaties (Kyoto). There is also one nation-state society, the USA, which enjoys exceptional centrality within most of the networks that criss-cross the globe (except curiously in the global game of football!).

Game critiques many of these existing globalization analyses by saying that 'this sort of [globalization] project is remarkably static and governed by a desire for stasis' (1998: 42). There is a tendency to treat the global as characterized by the current economic, social and political relations. However, this static view ignores what complexity also emphasizes. This is that the future is both unpredictable and yet irreversible. Will Hutton in *On the Edge* expresses the importance of such irreversibility when maintaining that 'change is all-encompassing and carries a new inevitability; its momentum is a superior power to any other, even that of the state . . . the force of change is irresistible' (Giddens and Hutton 2000: 2, 20, especially on non-linearity). For Hutton, global 'turbo-capitalism' is mobile and ruthless, driving all sorts of relations irreversibly and somewhat unpredictably onwards in terms of 'shareholder' interests.

Moreover, the notion of a global region implies distinct boundaries between what is global and what is its environment. This presumes a distinction between the global as essentially 'social' and the environment as essentially 'natural' (Macnaghten and Urry 1998). Complexity theory by contrast maintains that systems are always located within their environment and that there are complex entropic processes as a consequence. Analogously, 'global' processes should always be seen as social *and* physical, as 'material worlds'. There are no clear-cut and sustainable boundaries between global social relations *and* the environment within which they operate. There are material worlds with a complex irreversibility over time (see Latour 2000).

Much work within this 'regional' globalization paradigm also does not interrogate the iterative character of global systems. Their system characteristics are complexly generated from billions of actions occurring over multiple times. Hutton states that 'there *is* a phenomenon called globalisation' (Giddens and Hutton 2000: 23; emphasis added). But this does not do justice to the complicated and contingent array of processes occurring iteratively over time that can produce this in particular circumstances.

Hutton's argument that there simply *is* globalization is based upon the conventional distinction in the social sciences between what is 'structure' and what is 'agency'. Actions are normally seen as 'structurally' caused, such as by the capitalist structure, the patriarchal structure, the age structure and so on. Such a structure is 'ordered' and is reproduced. But, since social systems do change from time to time, the social sciences have had to draw upon the concept of agency to argue that some sets of human agents are able to 'escape' such structures and bring about change either individually (such as leaving a violent partner) or collectively through say class actions (such as the 1917 Bolshevik Revolution).

Giddens (1984), however, saw that this was not a satisfactory way of understanding the character of social life and social change. He developed the idea of a 'duality of structure' in order to overcome the limitations of the structure/agency divide. Important in this is the recursive character of social life. Giddens examines the temporal processes by which 'structures' are *both* drawn on to generate actions, and then are the unintended outcome of countless recursive actions by knowledgeable agents. So, rather than a dualism between structure and agency, there is seen to be a 'duality' in which structure and agency are bound up together and co-evolve over time (for counter-views, see Archer 1995; Mouzelis 1995).

However, Giddens insufficiently examines the 'complex' character of these structure–agency processes. Following the argument in the previous chapter, these processes are better understood through 'iteration' rather than 'recurrence'. It is iteration that means that the tiniest of 'local' changes can generate, over billions of repeated actions, unexpected, unpredictable and chaotic outcomes, sometimes the opposite of what agents thought they were trying to bring about (see Urry 2000b: ch. 8). Events are not 'forgotten' in such a system.

Such complex change may have nothing to do with agents seeking to change their particular world but stem from the emerging properties over time of the system as a whole. The agents may conduct what appear to be the same actions, indeed involving a constant imitation of the actions of others. But, because of the tiny modifications that occur in such actions, iteration can result in, through the irreversibility of time, transformations even in large-scale structures. Iteration produces, on occasions through dynamic emergence, non-linear changes and the sudden branching of the global order. So change can occur without a determining 'agency' producing different outcomes.

The character of such iterative social interactions has been likened to walking through a maze whose walls rearrange themselves as each new step is taken (Gleick 1988: 24). And as one walks, new sets of steps have to be made in order to adjust to the changing location of the surrounding walls of the maze.

In such iterations relationships are extremely sensitive to initial conditions. Small changes in one place (the equivalent of the butterfly's wings) can move the system into a completely different phase and a resulting bifurcation of the system. Byrne describes such large and non-linear outcomes as 'the last straw [that] breaks the camel's back' (1998: 170). They can produce radical regime change, such as the almost overnight implosion of the Soviet system following the 'small' event in 1989 of demolishing the Berlin Wall (I am unaware of complexity analyses of the collapse of the Soviet Empire).

More generally, Zohar and Marshall (1994), using notions from quantum physics, provide further criticism of the regional concepts of society and of the global. They develop and advocate the concept of *quantum society*, describing the collapse of the certainties of classical physics based upon the rigid categories of absolute time and space, solid impenetrable matter and strictly determinant laws of motion. As we saw in the previous chapter, the solid material objects of classical physics (and of society) dissolve at the subatomic level into wavelike patterns of probabilities, and these constitute probabilities of interconnections. Subatomic particles have no status as isolated entities but can be understood only as interconnections. Zohar and Marshall describe 'the strange world of quantum physics, an indeterminate world whose almost eerie laws mock the boundaries of space, time and matter' (1994: 33; see also Capra 1996: 30–1).

Zohar and Marshall develop analogies between the wave–particle effects within physics and varied characteristics of social life. They argue that

> Quantum reality . . . has the potential to be both particle-like and wave-like. Particles are individuals, located and measurable in space and time. They are either here or there, now and then. Waves [by contrast] are "non-local", they are spread out across all of space and time, and their instantaneous effects are everywhere. Waves extend themselves in every direction at once, they overlap and combine with other waves to form new realities (new emergent wholes).
> (Zohar and Marshall 1994: 326)

Social life can likewise be seen as simultaneously particle-like *and* wavelike. Such a notion is found in Henri Lefebvre's classic *The Production of Space* (1991). A house, he says, can be understood in two ways. Either it is stable and immovable with stark, cold and rigid outlines (as a 'particle'). It is the 'epitome of immovability', possessing clear and unambiguous boundaries (1991: 92). It is to think of a house as a very clear and distinct 'region', to return to Mol and Law's distinctions (1994). Alternatively the house can be thought of as a 'wave', as 'permeated from every direction by streams of energy which run in and out of it by every imaginable route'. In the latter the image of immovability is 'replaced by an image of a complex of mobilities, a nexus of in and out conduits', including visitors, electricity, water, sewerage, deliveries, gas, telephone/computer connections, radio and television signals and so on (Lefebvre 1991: 93; see also Roderick 1997; Urry 2000b: ch. 1).

Lefebvre also elaborates how commodities involve both moorings *and* mobile networks (or particles *and* waves). Commodities he says would have

> no 'reality' without such *moorings* or *points of insertion*, or without their existing as an ensemble . . . of stores, warehouses, ships, trains and trucks and the *routes* used. . . . Upon this basis are superimposed – in ways that transform, supplant or even threaten to destroy it – successive *stratified and tangled networks* which, though material in form, nevertheless have an existence beyond their materiality: paths, roads, railways, telephone links, and so on. (Lefebvre 1991: 402–3, emphasis added; see chapter 7 below).

Conclusion

In the next chapter I develop these arguments, especially drawing out how various global systems can be seen as both wave- *and* particle-like. We should analyse, first, global *waves*. Through iteration over irreversible times 'new emergent wholes' get generated. And, second, we need to examine how such waves are made up of countless individual *particles*, of people, social groups and networks that are resolutely 'located and measurable in space and time'. In later chapters I examine the very fixities in time and space that enable such mobilities – indeed, the more mobile the 'entity' in question the larger and more extensive the immobilities.

This distinction between global waves and particles breaks with the relatively immobile and fixed notion both of society and especially of the global criticized in this chapter. Material practices are simultaneously particle-like and wavelike, moored and mobile. Their analysis demands a set of concepts that properly capture their complex, emergent characteristics that take us beyond the notion of the global as 'region' criticized here. This notion stems from the application of the relatively conventional category of region to examine the extremely unconventional phenomena of emergent global systems. In the next chapter I turn to some of these systems, analysed through what I call globally integrated networks and global fluids.

4

Networks and Fluids

Metaphors

I begin by briefly considering what is an appropriate metaphor for the current global age. Pre-modern societies were often thought of metaphorically in terms of various animals, as well as different sorts of agricultural work (many are still powerful today). In modern industrial societies, dominant metaphors were those of the clock, modern machinery (train, car, assembly line) and the photographic lens. The lens provided the metaphor for modern epistemology based on the central importance of 'seeing' the world (see Urry 2000b: chs 2, 4). With the camera lens there is a one-to-one relationship between each point on the object and each point on the image of the plate or film. The metaphor of the lens implies a sequence, a separation between the parts of the picture and the whole picture, and a relatively extended process through time by which the image is generated and represented (see Adam 1990: 159).

By contrast, the hologram is a plausible metaphor for a complex informational age. Information in a hologram is not located in a particular part of it. Rather, any part contains, implies and resonates information of the whole, what Bohm calls the 'implicate order' (cited in Baker 1993: 142). Hologram means 'writing the whole'. Thus the 'focus is not on individual particles in motion, crossing time and space in succession, but on how all the information implied within a hologram is gathered up simultaneously' as an emergent whole (Adam 1990: 159). In the hologram the language of separate causes and effects is inappropriate, since connections are simultaneous *and* instantaneous. Everything implies everything else and thus it is impossible to conceive of the separate, if interdependent, 'parts' of a hologram. So the hologram demonstrates that powerful emergent or wavelike properties are not derived from constituent parts, nor can it be reduced to such parts. The metaphor of the hologram captures how relations are instantaneous, simultaneous and networked.

Networks

In this chapter I examine various spatial topologies, all of which involve hologram-like emergent relations that operate in-and-across networks. The notion of network is also a dominant metaphor for global times, rather than say 'machine' (Kelly 1998; Rycroft and Kash 1999: 107). Indeed complexity-writer Capra argues that 'networks' are the key to late-twentieth-century advances in science concerned with investigating the 'web of life'. He maintains that: 'Whenever we look at life, we look at networks' (Capra 1996: 82). And, if we think that global networks are complex in order to combine say the 10 million components making up a space shuttle, then we should note that modelling weather involves about 1 million interdependent variables or that the human brain contains 10 billion nerve cells and 1,000 billion synapses (Casti 1994: ch. 3). Such networks, whether of the weather, the brain or economic and social life, comprise enormous numbers of messages that, like relations within the hologram, move in all directions simultaneously. I will consider a number of characteristics of such networks.

Initially, it is useful to note that there are three basic network topologies. First, there are line or chain networks with many nodes that are spread out in more or less linear fashion. Second, there are star or hub networks, where most important relationships move through a central hub or hubs. Third, there are all-channel networks, in which communications proceed in more or less all directions across the network simultaneously (see Arquilla and Ronfeldt 2001: 7–8). Networks also vary as to whether the ties within it are loosely coupled or strongly coupled, the latter being especially problematic, as we saw in chapter 2 in many safety systems (Perrow 1999).

There are both strong and weak ties in all networks, with Granovetter (1983) having shown that it is especially the extensive weak ties of acquaintanceship and informational flows that are particularly central to successful job searches (see also Burt 1992: 24–7). It is also argued that, where there are 'structural holes' in networks, then this allows particular opportunities for developing informational access and control (Burt 1992). Networks also vary as to whether obligations and reciprocities across the network members are one way or all ways. We should also distinguish between the connections within a network that are purely 'social', based upon face-to-face connections, and those that are mediated by various 'material worlds' such as telephones, media, computer networks and so on (Wellman 2001).

Networks also overlap and interconnect with other networks so producing what has come to be known as the strange phenomenon of 'it is a small world'. Watts argues that 'even when two people do *not* have a friend in common they are separated by only a short chain of intermediaries' (1999: 4). These distant connections are often crucial to the forming of trust across far-flung networks (see David Lodge's excoriating account (1983) of the academic 'small world'). In the following it is presumed that it can be established where one network ends and another begins. But the networked connectedness of social relationships that the 'small-world' phenomenon indicates shows that this is not at all simple and straightforward in many cases.

The power of any network can be said to stem from its size, as indicated by the number of nodes within it, by the density of networked connections between each node, and by the connections that the network has with other networks. Size is the most significant determinant, because the value of a network does not merely increase arithmetically as more nodes are connected. Rather, 'the sum value of a network increases as the *square* of the number of members' (Kelly 1998: 23; emphasis added). In other words, as the number of nodes increases one by one, there is an exponential increase in the overall value or power of the network. So adding a few more nodes, more weak ties, disproportionately increases the value of that network for all the existing 'members'. Size was particularly important in the early development of the Ethernet network, where a few extra participants significantly increased the value of the network for everyone. Likewise, phone companies disproportionately gained from even small increases in the number of network-users. And the value of *each* fax machine greatly increased every time a few more machines were purchased.

Kelly (1998: 25) thus describes how networks can generate massive non-linear increases in output. Networks 'drastically amplify small inputs' through long-term and often exponential 'increasing returns', especially where all-channel networks get extended technologically. Such non-linear outcomes are generated by a system moving across what Malcolm Gladwell (2000) terms 'tipping points'. Tipping points involve three notions: that events and phenomena are contagious, that little causes can have big effects, and that changes can happen not in a gradual linear way but dramatically at a moment when the system switches. He describes the consumption of fax machines or mobile phones, when at a moment the system switched and suddenly every office needed a fax machine or every mobile person needed a mobile phone. The key here is that wealth comes not from scarcity, as in conventional economics, but from abundance. Each fax machine is so much more valuable if everyone else also has a fax machine that enables new networked connections to form and extend themselves (Gladwell 2000: 272–3). The benefits of each extra fax machine are non-linear. The tipping point is reached and extraordinary benefits flow throughout the network.

The key to understanding this process is the idea of 'increasing returns' developed by Brian Arthur (Waldrop 1994). This is not what economists have normally understood by the notion of 'increasing economies of scale'. Such economies are those that result from and are found within a *single* organization, such as Ford. These economies within such single firms increase output and over a long time reduce the average costs of production, until such a point that further gains are no longer possible.

By contrast, the notion of 'increasing returns' involves exponential increases in output (and rewards or wealth) that are spread *throughout a network of relationships* within which a variety of enterprises are located and operate. It is the 'externalities' *across* the networked relationships that can produce spectacular non-linear increases in output and income (as with the humble fax machine). The 'network economy' changes how such economies and their rewards operate, on occasions spreading massive, non-linear gains and benefits, although there will be resulting losses and costs elsewhere in the system (Kelly 1998). There are increasing returns that result from improved coordination between entities and from the processes of organizational learning across the network (Rycroft and Kash 1999: ch. 9).

Increasing returns are an example of the complexity analysis of positive feedback mechanisms. Such positive feedback in the form of increasing returns can result in astonishing escalations of economic wealth (Waldrop 1994). An obvious example is the Internet revolution that emerged out of the 'small' local change of the invention of the first Web browser around 1994 and the unpredicted emergence of worldwide e-commerce (see Castells 2001). This emergence was fuelled by the break-up over the previous decade of existing regional and national markets and the proliferation of new networking capability (on an insider's view as to the difference the Internet makes, see Gates 1999). Over time networks may bear no tendency to equilibrium because of the importance of such positive feedback. Dynamic and irreversible change takes place over time, change that irreversibly and unpredictably takes such a system further from equilibrium, depending upon its particular topology.

Moreover, such increasing returns are connected with the theory of how patterns of socio-technical development are 'path dependent'. The notions of path dependence emphasize the importance over time of the ordering of events or processes. *Contra* linear models, the temporal patterning in which events or processes occur very significantly influences the way that they eventually turn out (Mahoney 2000: 536). Causation can indeed flow from contingent minor events to hugely powerful general processes that through increasing returns then get locked in over lengthy periods of time. 'History matters' in the processes of path-dependent developments (North 1990: 100).

This path dependence is typically established for small-scale, local reasons. Thus most famously the QWERTY keyboard of the typewriter was introduced in 1873 in order to slow down typists.

Such a layout meant that the typewriter keys would not jam if typists typed more slowly. However, once the keyboard layout had been established for such small-scale reasons in the late nineteenth century, this layout has then remained even with the massive technological changes in the late twentieth century in what a 'keyboard' is (see North 1990; Arthur 1994a).

More significant in its long-term effect has been the way in which in the 1890s the petroleum-based car came to dominate over fuel alternatives to power cars. At the time, both electric and steam power were almost certainly preferable fuel systems (Motavalli 2000). But the 'path dependence' of the petroleum-based car got locked in, although it was not technologically preferable. But once it was locked in, the rest is history, as an astonishing array of other industries, activities and interests came to mobilize around the petroleum-based car. As North writes more generally: 'Once a development path is set on a particular course, the network externalities, the learning process of organizations, and the historically derived subjective modelling of the issues reinforce the course' (1990: 99).

The key here is that 'small chance events become magnified by positive feedback' and this 'locks in' such systems, so that massive increasing returns or positive feedback result over time (Brian Arthur, cited in Waldrop 1994: 49; see also Mahoney 2000). Relatively deterministic patterns of inertia reinforce established patterns through processes of positive feedback. This escalates change through a 'lock-in' that over time takes the system away from what we might imagine to be the point of 'equilibrium' and from what could have been optimal in 'efficiency' terms, such as a non-QWERTY keyboard or electric forms of powering cars (Motavalli 2000).

It should not be thought that there is necessarily a single point of equilibrium that can be unambiguously specified as the most optimal (on 'sociological' path dependency, see Mahoney 2000). There are multiple equilibria and hence no simple move towards it that a system will generate. The importance, moreover, of the lock-in means that institutions matter a great deal to how systems develop. Such institutions can produce a long-term irreversibility that is 'both more predictable and more difficult to reverse' (North 1990: 104). The effects of the petroleum car over a century after its chance establishment is the best example of how difficult it is to reverse locked-in institutional processes (see Sheller and Urry 2000).

Positive feedbacks and path dependence, where contingent events can set in motion institutional patterns with deterministic outcomes, are central to the power of various networks operating across the globe. Such global networks are large in size, will involve dense interactions within their nodes and will interact with other networks, so further expanding their exceptional range and influence. They do not derive directly and uniquely from human intentions and actions. Humans are intricately networked *with* machines, texts, objects and other technologies. There are no purified *social* networks, only 'material worlds' that involve peculiar and complex socialities *with* objects (Latour 1993; Knorr-Cetina 1997).

Such networks thus involve an array of new *machines and technologies* that extend them in time–space. These include fibre-optic cables, jet planes, audio-visual transmissions, digital TV, computer networks, satellites, credit cards, faxes, electronic point-of-sale terminals, portable phones, electronic stock exchanges, high-speed trains, virtual reality, nuclear, chemical and conventional military technologies and weapons, new waste products and health risks. These machines and technologies generate new fluidities of astonishing speed and scale (on the 'nanosecond nineties', see Peters 1992).

These scapes help to constitute different forms of networked relationships across the globe. But I have so far used the term 'network' or 'networked' to refer to a wide array of very different systems. It was noted in chapter 1 how Castells likewise uses 'network' to refer to varied processes that should be distinguished from one another. So to capture these different modes of 'networked relationships', I distinguish between *globally integrated networks* (GINs) and *global fluids* (GFs; see chapter 3 above; Mol and Law 1994; Law and Mol 2000). In the next section I examine the nature of GINs.

Globally Integrated Networks

GINs consist of complex, enduring and predictable networked connections between peoples, objects and technologies stretching across multiple and distant spaces and times (Law 1994: 24; Murdoch 1995: 745). Relative distance is a function of the relations between the components comprising that network. The invariant outcome of a network, such as that for anaemia testing in the Netherlands, is delivered across its entirety in ways that often overcome regional boundaries. Things are made *close* through these networked relations. Such a network of technologies, skills, texts and brands, a global hybrid, ensures that the same 'service' or 'product' is delivered in more or less the same way across the entire network. Such products are predictable, calculable, routinized and standardized.

There are many 'global' enterprises organized through GINs. Examples include McDonald's, American Express, Coca-Cola, Microsoft, Sony, Greenpeace, Manchester United and so on. Each involves global networks. 'McDonaldization', as this has been termed, involves companies on a global scale organized with a minimum of central organization (see Ritzer 1992, 1997, 1998). McDonaldization produces new kinds of low-skilled standardized jobs especially for young people (McJobs), new products that radically alter people's eating habits, and new social habits worldwide, such as eating standardized fast food from take-away restaurants ('grazing').

Indeed, most of the transnational companies currently roaming the planet are organized through GINs. These 'organizations' generally produce few 'failings' across the network. In part such a network exists to counter the often extraordinarily turbulent environment within which they operate. Such networks, with more or less instantaneous and simultaneous communications, enable the brand, associated products and modes of service to roam in much the same form across the surface of the earth (on global brands, see Klein 2000; Sklair 2001).

Sometimes there is limited adaptation to local circumstances, as with McDonald's in east Asia. But, even if local owner-operators are involved in day-to-day management, the global network in the end wins out (on how Big Macs do all taste the same, see Watson 1997: 22). The Managing Director of McDonald's in Singapore explains as follows: 'McDonald's sells . . . a system, not products.' This 'system' is taught at Hamburger University and systematized in the 600-page *Operations and Training Manual* (Watson 1997: 21). Certain key features of the global network include not only standardized products but also the standardized and monitored 'smiling service' to strangers. Such GINs produce not only predictable material goods and services, but also calculable and controllable simulations of 'experiences' apparently 'more real than the original' (Baudrillard 1983; Eco 1986; Ritzer 1997; Rifkin 2000).

GINs can also be found within some oppositional organizations such as Greenpeace. Like other global players, Grenpeace devotes much attention to developing and sustaining its brand identity throughout the world. Greenpeace's brand identity has 'such an iconic status that it is a world-wide symbol of ecological virtue quite above and beyond the actual practical successes of the organisation' within various societies (Szerszynski 1997: 46).

These global networks are significantly 'deterritorialized'. They move in and through places in ways that transform and distort time and space. Such networks constitute one of most powerful sets of 'particles' comprising the new world order. They are massively powerful, particularly because of their mobility, their networked character, their capacity to generate increasing returns from the use and exploitation of their global brand and their endogenous self-organizing character (Klein 2000).

Such GINs show three weaknesses. First, since a set of networked organizations can generate much greater increasing returns than can single companies, so these individual companies can be outperformed in the global marketplace, as IBM was in the case of personal computers.

Second, the power of a global brand based within a GIN can evaporate almost overnight from quite minor occurrences. The brand of Monsanto disappeared because of the company's association with producing genetically modified food. Indeed, the more powerful the brand, the more there is to lose. Klein (2000) shows just how extensive are the various resistances to global brands carried along the scapes of the emergent global order. I examine below the complex nature of scandals that can result in massive consequences for individual GINs such as Arthur Andersen, the paper-shredding auditors of Enron.

And, third, these single companies can be very brittle and lack the capacity to bend with rapidly changing circumstances. They may not be quite like the former East European command economies, but their lack of 'fluidity' and 'flexibility' may mean that they are very vulnerable to fluid changes in desire, taste and style that leave them struggling to catch up. On occasions such companies are insufficiently fluid to implement appropriate organizational learning (see Rycroft and Kash 1999).

In the next sections I turn to some other global hybrids, GFs, which are much more 'liquid' in character.

Global Fluids

Emile Durkheim criticized the fluid, unstable, non-authoritative character of 'sensuous representations'. Sensuous representations 'are in a perpetual flux; they come after each other likes the waves of a river, and even during the time that they last, they do not remain the same thing' (Durkheim 1915/1968: 433). What is required for science, according to Durkheim, is to abstract from these flows of time and space in order to arrive at concepts that are proper 'collective representations'. Durkheim sees concepts as lying beneath the shifting perpetual, sensuous surface flux. Concepts are outside time and change. They do not move by themselves. They are fixed and immutable and it is the task of science to reveal them. Science involves not being seduced by the endlessly changing 'sensations, perceptions and images' that lie on the surface (Durkheim 1915/1968: 432–4).

However, I dissent from this 'structural' view of concepts. The development of a 'mobile sociology' demands metaphors that do view social and material life as being 'like the waves of a river'. Such fluid notions are necessary to capture those multiple transformations of collective representations in which 'collective' relations are no longer societal and structural. Many contemporary writers are developing and elaborating various fluid metaphors to capture aspects of contemporary social life, of the sea, rivers, flux, waves and liquidity (Bachelard 1942/1983; Urry 2000b). Williams describes latent 'structures of feeling' as being a social experience that is 'in solution' (1977: 133–4). Castells (1996) talks of the 'power of flows'. Appadurai (1996) argues for the metaphors of 'flow', 'uncertainty' and 'chaos' and Deleuze and Guattari (1986, 1988) talk of bodies in a vortex. Shields (1997) maintains that flows should be seen as a whole new paradigm. White (1992) characterizes the social world as constituted by disorderly and sticky 'gels and goos'. Mol and Law (1994) generally elaborate a 'fluid spatiality' (see also Sheller 2000).

So what then is meant here by the notion of *global* fluid? First, while fluids undoubtedly involve networks, such a notion does not do justice to the uneven, emergent and unpredictable shapes that such fluids may take. Also such fluids are partially structured by the various 'scapes' of the global order, the networks of machines, technologies, organizations, texts and actors that constitute various interconnected nodes along which flows can be relayed (Graham and Marvin 2001). Global fluids travel along these various scapes, but they may escape, rather like white blood corpuscles, through the 'wall' into surrounding matter and effect unpredictable consequences upon that matter. Fluids move according to certain novel shapes and temporalities as they break free from the linear, clock time of existing scapes – but they cannot go back, they cannot return, because of the irreversibility of time.

Such fluids of diverse viscosity organize the messy power of complexity processes (see Kelly 1995). They result from people acting upon the basis of local information but where these local actions are, through countless iteration, captured, moved, represented, marketed and generalized within multiple global waves, often impacting upon hugely distant places and peoples. The 'particles' of people, information, objects, money, images, risks and networks move within and across diverse regions forming heterogeneous, uneven, unpredictable and often unplanned waves (see Urry 2000b). Such waves demonstrate no clear point of departure, deterritorialized movement, at certain speeds and at different levels of viscosity with no necessary end state or purpose. This means that such fluids create over time their own context for action rather than being seen as 'caused' by such a context. These global fluid systems are in part self-organizing, creating and maintaining boundaries.

I now describe some such GFs. In the next chapter I develop a complexity analysis that shows the irreversible and non-linear intersections that occur between such GFs as they spread over, through and under multiple times and spaces. GFs are shown in that chapter to be utterly crucial categories of analysis in the globalizing social world that have in part rendered both regions and networks less causally powerful.

Travelling peoples

Travelling peoples move along various transportation scapes. At the beginning of the twenty-first century there are well over 700 million movements across international borders each year (compared with twenty-five million in 1950); at any time 300,000 passengers are in flight *above* the USA, equivalent to a substantial city; there are thirty-one million refugees and 100 million international migrants worldwide; and international travel, which constitutes the largest movement of people across borders that has ever occurred, accounts for over one-twelfth of world trade (Makimoto and Manners 1997: ch. 1; Papastergiadis 2000: 10, 41, 54; WTO 2000). A crucial component of this fluid is made up of the transnational capitalist class, whose pampered routeways of travel between the major industrial, financial and service hubs shows by far the greatest density (on the life of this class, see Sklair 2001).

This fluid of travelling peoples involves almost everywhere across the globe (with published travel statistics for over 190 countries). It involves people travelling for work-related reasons, legal and increasingly illegal, those travelling for leisure and pleasure, again legally and illegally, those travelling as refugees or asylum-seekers, and those being smuggled voluntarily as migrants and involuntarily as short-term and disposable slaves. The most rapidly growing form of smuggling is that of human beings moved often across hugely policed and effective borders, with an associated growth in the international 'slave' trade. There are thought to be more slaves now than at the height of the eighteenth-century slave trade (Bales 1999: 9).

Such very different travelling peoples intermittently encounter each other within the 'non-places of modernity', the airport lounge, the coach station, the motorway service area and so on (Augé 1995; although 'business lounges' separate off the transnational capitalist class from most other travellers). These different peoples also overlap, with one category dissolving into another, giving rise not just to the travelling of peoples but also to diverse, complex and hard-to-categorize 'travelling cultures' (see Clifford 1997; Rojek and Urry 1997). Moreover, while there are 200 nation states, there are at least 2,000 'nation peoples', all of which experience various kinds of displacement, movement and ambiguous location (R. Cohen 1997: pp. ix–x). The most striking of such 'societies' formed through the global fluid of travelling peoples is the 'overseas Chinese' (R. Cohen 1997: ch. 4; Ong and Nonini 1997). Such massive, hard-to-categorize, contemporary migrations, often with oscillatory flows between unexpected locations, have been described through the language of the 'new physics'. These migration patterns are to be seen as a series of turbulent waves, with a hierarchy of eddies and vortices, with globalism a virus that stimulates resistance, and the migration system a cascade moving away from any apparent state of equilibrium (Papastergiadis 2000: 102–4, 121).

The Internet

This rather obscure technology, designed by the American defence intelligence in the 1970s and 1980s, unpredictably resulted in an astonishing system of many-to-many communications across the globe. The transformation of this distributed, horizontal military-based system into the huge global Internet stemmed from various small-scale changes made by American scientific and research networks and from counter-cultural efforts to produce a computer network that possessed horizontal public access (students 'invented' the modem in 1978 and the Mosaic web browser in 1992: Rushkoff 1994). Castells notes: 'the openness of the system also results from the constant process of innovation and free accessibility enacted by early computer hackers and the network hobbyists who still populate the net by the thousands' (1996: 356).

The Internet did not originate within the business world, nor from within any single state bureaucracy (see Castells's brilliant history: 2001). In significant ways its users are key producers of the very technology. The autopoeitic, self-organizing character of the Internet is described as follows:

No central hub or command structure has constructed it. . . . It has installed none of the hardware on which it works, simply hitching a largely free ride on existing computers, networks, switching systems, telephone lines. This was one of the first systems to present itself as a multiplicitous, bottom-up, piecemeal, self-organizing network which . . . could be seen to be emerging without any centralized control. (Plant 1997: 49)

The Internet is also the best example of how technology invented for one purpose, military communication in the event of a nuclear attack, unpredictably and irreversibly evolved through iteration and a path dependence into purposes unintended and undreamt of by its early developers. It has resulted in a massive worldwide activity, with sixteen million users in 1995, 400 million users in early 2001, and a projected one billion by 2005 (Castells 2001: 3). Information on the Internet doubles every few months (Brand 1999: 14, 87). An awesome pattern of path dependence has been laid down, a pattern analysed by Castells as the 'winner-takes-all system that characterizes business competition in the new economy' (2001: 100).

The Internet enables horizontal communication that cannot be effectively surveilled, controlled or censored by national societies. It possesses an 'elegant, non-hierarchical rhizomatic global struc-ture' (Morse 1998: 187) and is based upon lateral, horizontal *hyper-text* links that render the boundaries between objects within the archive as endlessly fluid (Featherstone 2000: 187). The Internet can be seen as a metaphor for social life that is fluid, involving thou-sands of networks, of people, machines, programmes, texts and images in which quasi-subjects and quasi-objects mix together in new hybrid forms. Ever-new computer networks and links prolif-erate mostly in unplanned and mixed patterns. Such a fluid space is a world of *mixtures*. Messages 'find their way', rather like blood through multiple capillaries. Fluids can get around absences. Such computer networks are not solid or stable and are contingent. Hypertext programmes and the Net comprise 'webs of footnotes without central points, organizing principles, hierarchies' (Plant 1997: 10; see also chapter 3 below). Such digitized information 'efface[s] the difference between cause and effect, ends and means, subject and object, active and passive' (Luke 1995: 97).

Information

This GF is intimately connected with the Internet, as 'knowledge' has been 'informationalized'. Knowledge was once found in specific form (the manuscript, the book, the map), located in particular places (archives, museums, libraries) and embodied within the minds of certain people (scholars, archivists, mapmakers). Such relatively fixed repositories of knowledge could be destroyed or killed. Books, manuscripts, paintings and maps, indeed whole libraries such as that at Alexandria, could be burnt and the knowledge would physically disappear (Brand 1999: ch. 12).

But knowledge is now transmutating into digitized information (Featherstone 2000). This shows the significance of *material* worlds, hybrids that combine objects, texts, technologies and bodies, to transmit around the globe tiny weightless bits of information. Analysis of either the physical *or* the social elements of such a shift would be on its own meaningless. And nature itself is being transformed into genetic codes that are owned, accessed and circulated socially, with the growth of the 'informational body' (Franklin et al. 2000: 128–9).

Further, this change can be appreciated through a shifting metaphor, from the stationary, wooden, fixed 'desk' occupied by the individual scholar (even with chained books in the medieval period), to the ephemeral, mobile and interchangeable 'desktop' that can be occupied by anyone. Or there is the shift from the specific religious 'icon' to the ubiquitous and instantaneously recognized computer 'icon'. With digitization, information adopts patterns and modes of mobility that are substantially separate from material form or presence (Hayles 1999: 18–20). Information is everywhere (and nowhere), travelling (more or less) instantaneously along the fluid networks of global communications. Its repositories cannot be burnt down as with the medieval library, although particular computers can (will!) have their memories wiped.

The exceptional growth of networked, spatially indifferent, information is transforming commerce and work partly because of the difficulty of charging for digitized information that is ephemeral and fluid (Castells 1996). This fluid of information is transforming education and science because of the exponential and irreversible growth in the sheer amount and complexity of scientific information (Rescher 1998: ch. 4; Urry 2002a). More generally, the 'new artificial life-form' of the global telecommunications *Matrix*' has been described as 'nonlinear, asymmetrical, chaotically-assembled' (Imken 1999: 92). The media are 'migratory', with both viewers and images in simultaneous circulation and recirculation. Neither fit into circuits or audiences bound to a local or a national space (Appadurai 1996).

Wars have consequently turned into 'virtual wars', at least for those controlling the virtual weaponry. Such 'virtual wars' appear 'to take place on a screen. . . . War affords the pleasures of a spectacle. . . . When war becomes a spectator sport, the media becomes the decisive theatre of operations' (Ignatieff 2000: 191). And warfare more generally is being networked and informationalized, with the emergence of 'network centric warfare' and what Arquilla and Ronfeldt (2001) call 'netwars' often occurring between non-state actors.

World money

Strange (1986) describes this GF as being a kind of 'casino capitalism', detached, self-organizing and operating beyond both individual national economies and the specific industries and services involved in world production and trade (see also Castells 1996; Leyshon and Thrift 1997). Daily foreign-exchange dealings are worth sixty times more than the daily value of world exports (Held et al. 1999: 209; the ratio grew fivefold between 1979 and 1995). Money is traded for money especially in terms of its future values. Such a GF is organized through 'just-in-time 24-hour networks'. It involves calculations of, and bets on, hugely uncertain futures: 'traders are trading in time itself, which is to say in the momentary forward fluctuations of price and value. The latter are . . . expressions of the most abstract sort: of money itself and, even more abstractly, of the price of money at some future point in time' (Boden 2000: 189).

This commodification of the future generates extraordinarily fluid movements across, and beyond, the regions and networks in which money has been organized and regulated. There is extensive movement of money into 'offshore' locations designed to minimize taxes and to facilitate the laundering of illegal funds. Martin and Schumann (1997) describe the consequences in complexity terms. They say that the 'abandonment of (border) controls on capital has therefore set up a dynamic which, by systematically nullifying the sovereignty of nations, has long been seen to have disastrously anarchic implications' (Martin and Schumann 1997: 61) At the same time the national controls are themselves now sources of financial gain since 'any nation's financial controls appear to be made for the sole purpose of being evaded' (Eatwell and Taylor 2000: 37; all emphasized in the original).

Moreover, recent decades have seen the 'firewalls' between different financial markets dissolve. As a consequence, 'all segments of the system are now tightly interdependent' so that 'microeconomic responses can easily escalate into macroeconomic *contagion*' (Eatwell and Taylor 2000: 45; emphasis added). This results in the extreme price swings that occur within global financial markets, especially where so-called derivative trading is involved. These financial instruments, developed to manage the risk that the financial system has itself created, in turn produce new systemic risks. Price movements rapidly move away from equilibrium, stemming from 'the cumulative effect of a beauty contest [that] may result in massive concentrations of extreme price swings' (Eatwell and Taylor 2000: 103; and, on the role of contagion in 'tipping points', see Gladwell 2002).

Thus, not only is money highly fluid but so too are global financial crises. Eatwell and Taylor talk of the 'recent crisis in Asia and its *contagious* spread to Russia, South Africa, and Latin America' (2000: 26; emphasis added). And so far there is no international body effecting global financial regulation of such fluidities and the resulting 'prevalence of contagion', the lack of negative feedback mechanisms and the potential of the whole system to 'self-destruct'. The proposed Tobin tax of 1 per cent that would be levied on all foreign currency transactions is indeed designed to slow down the contagious effects of such global fluidities (Martin and Schumann 1997: 82).

Global brands or logos

Global brands or logos increasingly roam the globe. They are enormously powerful and ubiquitous. They result from how the most successful corporations have shifted from manufacturing products to becoming brand producers. Their fluid-like power stems from marketing, design, sponsorship, public relations and advertising expenditures, with such companies becoming 'economies of signs'. Such brands include Nike, Apple, Gap, Pepsi-Cola, Benetton, Body Shop, Virgin, Swatch, Calvin Klein, Sony, Starbucks and so on.

Central to the branding process is the 'global teen market', with about one billion young people disproportionately consuming similar consumer brands from across the globe, even within mainland China. MTV, the key scape of this global teen market, broadcast in eighty-three countries in 1999 (Klein 2000: 118–21).

Products thus are the effect of the brand rather than the brand being the effect of the product (Franklin et al. 2000: 168–9). The brand creates and maintains links amongst very different products. They thus produce 'concepts' or 'lifestyles': 'liberated from the real-world burdens of stores and product manufacturing, these brands are free to soar, less as the dissemination of goods and services than as collective hallucinations' (Klein 2000: 22). The power of such fluid-like brands is essentially 'cultural', not residing in the workplaces, workforces or the objects produced and sold (whether these are running shoes, body lotions, aircraft journeys or sweaters).

In the case of Nike, a 'company that swallows cultural space in giant gulps', there is an enormous 'power of the swoosh', a literally free-floating signifier (Goldman and Papson 1998; Klein 2000: 51). And this power is insidious, seeping into diverse 'cultural' domains as each brand replicates through cloning. As for Body Shop and Starbucks, 'they had fostered powerful identities by making their brand concept into a virus and sending it out into the culture via a variety of channels: cultural sponsorship, political controversy, the consumer experience and brand extensions' (Klein 2000: 21).

Moreover, brands do not just seep downwards, since they often emerge from street life and culture, urban black youth, New Age, political protest, labour movement, Green critiques and so on. Brands are powerful concepts, but they are always on the move, often ironically flowing in and out of cultures including cultures of protest. Indeed, almost every organization is affected by, and becomes an element within, this branding global fluid, with universities, NGOs, governments, artists, charities, political parties, hospitals, architects and so on all increasingly part of the branded life.

Such brands demonstrate increasing returns; they magnify and expand their power through use, time and time and time again. Their power does not get used up but multiplies. The power, range and ubiquity of such brands are expanded even when they are subject to massive political protest, as with the intense campaigns over Nike's use of sweatshop labour. Brands then have become super-territorial and super-organic, floating free and constituting a 'defining medium of exchange in global nature, global culture' (Franklin et al. 2000: 182).

Automobility

This GF of immense consequence could almost be seen as 'viral', taking off in North America and then virulently spreading into, and taking over, most parts of the body social within all corners of the globe. Such physical mobilities are environmentally costly, with transport accounting for one-third of CO_2 emissions. World car travel is predicted to triple between 1990 and 2050, there are well over half a billion cars roaming the globe, and many new countries, such as China, are developing an 'automobile culture'. By 2030 there may be one billion cars worldwide (Motavalli 2000: 20–1).

The fluid of automobility uniquely combines the quintessential manufactured object of industrial societies (the petroleum car), the major system of individual ownership after housing, an extraordinarily powerful machinic complex linked to most other industrial and service sectors, the dominant form of quasi-private mobility that subordinates almost all other mobilities, the leading culture defining the nature of the 'good life' through possessing a car, the single most important form of resource use, and the main determinant of time fragmentation, as multitasking comes to characterize much social life (Sheller and Urry 2000). Slater points out that the key here is not the 'car' as such but the system of fluid interconnections: 'a car is not a car because of its physicality but because systems of provision and categories of things are "materialized" in a stable form' (2001: 6).

The fluid of automobility combines the notion of the autonomous self with that of a machine with the capacity for autonomous movement along the paths, lanes, streets and routeways of one society after society. It is a self-organizing, non-linear system spreading cars, car-drivers, roads, petroleum supplies and a huge array of novel objects, technologies and signs that petroleum-and-steel cars presuppose and endlessly reproduce.

As I noted above, the GF of automobility stemmed from the path-dependent pattern laid down from the end of the nineteenth century. Once economies and societies were 'locked in' to the fluid of automobility, then massive increasing returns resulted for those producing and selling the petroleum car and its associated infrastructure, products and services. And at the same time social life got locked in to the mode of individualized mobility that automobility generates and presupposes. This is, of course, a mode of individualized mobility that is neither socially necessary nor inevitable but one that seems impossible to break from (but see Hawken et al. 1999).

Environmental and health hazards

These hazards travel both geographically and temporally in non-linear, unpredictable and irreversible fashion. For example, BSE takes between five and twenty years to incubate, nuclear accidents can affect generations that are not yet born, nuclear radiation can survive for thousands of years, hormone-disrupting chemicals appear to affect species living across all parts of the globe, and no one knows what the environmental consequences will be in various unimaginable futures of the widespread planting of GM crops. Such fluid, moving hazards, which start locally, roam over the globe, producing consequences that are un-measurable and indeed 'invisible' in time–space (see Adam 1998: 25–7, 35; 2000). Colborn et al. summarize the globally fluid and complex nature of these processes: 'We design new technologies at a dizzying pace and deploy them on an unprece-dented scale around the world long before we can begin to fathom their possible impact on the global system or ourselves' (1996: 244; see also Beck 1992; Adam et al. 2000). And, if there is one sure lesson here, it is that the physical world is as dynamic, cos-mopolitan and productive of emergent effects as is the social world (Clark 2000).

Thus it was only a small local research project begun in a Hawaiian hut in 1958 that 'accidentally' revealed the awesomely significant and probably irreversible forty-year increase in green-house gases (Brand 1999: 138). The results of the Mauna Loa CO_2 records have then come to play a central role in the performance of what is now seen as a 'global nature', a nature regarded as subject to exceptionally hazardous and irreversible levels of threat stretching over an immensely lengthy period (in what I term 'glacial time' (Urry 2000b)).

The world's oceans

These might be viewed as an almost literal global fluid. Oceans are increasingly seen as possessing life-making properties and with levels of biodiversity that may help to 'save the globe' from some the hazards just outlined (see Helmreich 2000). Bioprospecting the life-making attributes of the sea, such as the curiously liminal coral reefs, involves mobile networks of re-searchers, government funding (especially from the USA), notions of biodiversity, commercial companies and freezing in the form of patents. In particular: 'The marine environment . . . is being uploaded into a world wide web which reconstitutes biodiversity . . . as a "life" force to be plugged into projects of healing for individuals and "sustainable" use of the planet' (Helmreich 2000: 26).

Such oceanic networks, under the guise of saving the individ-ual and the globe, roam the global commons, bioprospecting the oceans for patentable properties, as life has come to be viewed as a 'network of salty fluids' (Helmreich 2000: 28). One of these webs of relationships, the Monterey Bay Aquarium Research Institute, is a leader in the use of deep robotics and of telepresent technologies of visualization of the deep oceans.

Social movements

Many commentators have begun to characterize social movements as fluid-like with the exceptional and unexpected upsurges of protest. Biggs (1998) describes rapid mobilization as involving endogenous, self-reinforcing processes where a small initial change is amplified by 'positive feedback'. This produces a 'contagion effect' significant within many protest movements where strikes or other actions spread like 'forest fires'. McKay (1998: 52) similarly talks of anarchist movements as ebbing and flowing, grouping and regrouping. Jasper (1997) describes the flows, webs and networks that are involved in many forms of artful protest (see also Jordan 1998).

Overall, Melucci describes movements of protest as involving 'an amorphous nebula of indistinct shape and variable density' (1996: 113–14). Sheller (2000) shows how these uncertain interactions and dynamic change involved in 'social movements' should be analysed through the prism of non-Euclidean sticky spaces and bending times. Social movements often demonstrate movement with no beginning or end point. Movements flow along various channels but may 'overflow' or 'ebb away'. They can be more or less viscous, especially as public domains can enable cascades of action. Multiple temporalities are involved, particularly as the particles in a movement may be transformed into powerful waves. Various kinds of 'free space' can enable movements to seep through borders and boundaries, reappearing in different guises, especially within unexpected locations. Such social movements always involve the physical movements of peoples, vehicles, texts, objects, information and so on that coalesce and disperse, concentrate and dissolve, pouring around barriers, switching the point of attack and intermittently flooding various spaces (Sheller 2000; on 'network switchings', see White 1995).

A protest in London in 1999 is described as follows: 'the movement baffled the police efforts to find its center, its motive force, its central governors; instead, from the pond emerged a plague of crawling, mobile "slugs" – flowing over the surface of London's squares, roads, and bridges' (Sheller 2000: 24; on 'cellular slime mold', see Fox Keller 1985: ch. 5). Likewise in late 2000, a mere 2,000 people protesting against high petrol taxes almost brought all economic activity in Britain to a halt. For a couple of weeks these protestors blocked the relatively few localized nodes where the just-in-time delivery of petrol for cars and lorries commenced. The protestors brought a large economy 'to its knees'. This was achieved through a loose network of highly mobile and connected (through their mobile phones) protestors with no evident leaders to arrest and no clear organization that the police could raid or sue. The fluidity of the petrol supply turned out to be immensely susceptible to particular points of blockage by fluidly organized protestors. These were also very adept at getting their message and appropriate images onto the world's media, although much of this media skill was learnt during the very course of the protest itself. They thus learnt from and contributed to the analogous mobile protesting occurring at the same time across Western Europe. A tiny cause (2,000 protestors) thus chaotically produced, because of certain patterns of localized refining, just-in-time delivery, instantaneous real-time communications, globalized media and motorized mobility, influential protest that disrupted centre-left governments across much of Europe.

Overall, Arquilla and Ronfeldt summarize the nature of social movements and 'netwars' within an age of complexity: 'Information-age threats are more likely to be more diffuse, dispersed, multi-dimensional, non-linear, and ambiguous than industrial-age threats. Metaphorically, then, future conflicts may resemble the Oriental game of Go more than the western game of chess' (2001: 2).

I have thus set out some strikingly powerful fluid systems. Together with GINs, these fluids roam the lands, the seas and inner and outer space, or what we metaphorically term the 'globe' (Ingold 1993). These systems travel along and beyond various scapes intersecting with each other in complex, unpredictable and time–space compressed forms. Various times are folded into these roaming hybrids, including nanosecond instantaneity (as with the Internet), commodified futures (global money), the hyper-fragmentation of time (with automobility) and awesome longevity (with the oceans). They roam the globe, possessing the power of rapid movement, across, over and under many apparent regions, disappearing and then reappearing, transmutating their form, cropping up like the islands of an archipelago, unexpectedly and chaotically. They can appear both horizontally but also vertically, arriving in the case of international terrorists not from the wild zones of the subways of New York, but also astonishingly from the air as planes or as biomaterials.

Moreover, extraordinarily rapid and unexpected switches, or 'zapping' (Emirbayer and Mische 1998) or 'turning points' (Abbott 2001) occur between such fluids as they pass into, through, over and under each other. Central to many of these switches or zappings between the GFs are various kinds of software increasingly infused into the very fabric of everyday life (Thrift 2001). Such pervasive computing has largely remained opaque and uncontested. And yet software is everywhere producing switching and mobility between different fluids, through the Internet with its massive search engines, databases of information storage and retrieval, world money flows, especially through the ubiquitous 'spreadsheet culture', intelligent transport systems, robotic vision machines under the oceans, and vision machines more generally. It was calculated that in 1996 there were some seven billion software systems (Thrift 2001: 18).

Finally, these complex intersections between fluid spatialities suggest a further metaphor, what Law and Mol term 'fire' (2000). By this they try to capture how a continuity of shape can be the very effect of movement, even of abrupt and discontinuous movement (note the previous description of gases). The term also emphasizes how there is a striking dependence of presence upon what happens to be absent. Indeed, more generally social life often depends upon peculiar combinations of the presence and the absence. 'Fire' also brings out how the forms of absence that constitute a present are themselves patterned (they discuss a star pattern but there are others). There is thus a complex oscillating pattern of presence and absence, of contradictions, within social phenomena. There are not fixed entities with stable attributes (Abbott 2001: 40–1).

This concept of fire characterizes contemporary communications. In intimate and unexpected forms, an array of technical and instrumental means of communications are combined with humans. They have partially replaced the spatiality of 'co-present sociality' with new modes of present and absent 'strangerness'

(Bogard 1996, 2000). Such machinic hybrids involve a profound strangeness. There is 'a contradiction between nearness and remoteness, or mobility and fixation. . . . Cyberspace communications, in a word, are strange – at the push of a button, territories dissolve, oppositions of distant and close, motion and stasis, inside and out, collapse; identities are marginalized and simulated, and collectivities lose their borders' (Bogard 2000: 28).

There are now almost always 'strangers' in our midst – on TV, the computer, the mobile phone. There is a curious 'flickering' combination of presence and absence. Bogard characterizes such a collapse of distance as an impure or indeterminate relationship, neither one nor two, as a fractal space: 'this blurring of boundaries between the monad and the dyad is an excellent image of the rapidly evolving symbiosis of bodies and computers, groups and communications networks, societies and cybernetic systems' (Bogard 2000: 40). The cyborg is neither a single monad nor a dyad. It is simultaneously private and public, intimate and distant. Global relations thus involve new fractal social spaces, as each realm folds over, under, through and beyond each other in striking new social topologies. These are 'firelike', oscillatory, flickering, both here and there, both inside and outside rather like a Mobius strip (Bogard 1996: 29; see the related critique of general linear reality in Abbott 2001).

Conclusion

I have thus examined a variety of metaphors to capture the complex character of systems operating in some sense globally. I have especially considered the key notion in complexity of 'network' and made a number of points about their systemic patterning in the social sphere. I especially considered how increasing returns and path dependence are central to explaining the astonishing power of certain networks.

I dealt specifically with two kinds of networked systems, GINs and GFs. Various examples of each of these have been elaborated, especially showing how GFs are powerful mobile entities that are not exactly here or there, moving rather like waves through the social order. I have presumed that in an era in which there are few if any social phenomena that possess fixed and stable attributes then complexity is the appropriate theoretical resource to make sense of their fluid and systemic characteristics.

In the next chapter I examine more systematically the nature of the global relationships that are made up of complex intersections between these various globally networked systems, of networks and fluids. I particularly deploy the mathematical notion of the 'attractor' to explain why systems only move within certain 'spaces' within the entire field of global possibilities.

5

Global Emergence

Emergent Effects and the 'Local'

The social sciences have wrestled with competing claims that there either are, or are not, properties of the social world that can be reduced to the characteristics of individuals that make up that world. Such debate has perhaps generated more heat than light and I will not spend too long adding to that heat.

I presume from the discussion of complexity that there are indeed emergent properties at the collective level. To reduce that level to 'facts about individuals' would be to lose important knowledge of those emergent properties. And, anyway, there is no effective way of characterizing 'individuals' without describing various social linkages that make up those very emergent properties.

I have already noted how the complexity sciences have examined the emergent character of various populations. I have shown the limitations of science that reduces complex phenomena to linear causes. Cohen and Stewart talk of those 'regularities of behaviour that somehow seem to transcend their own ingredients' (1994: 232; see also chapter 2 above). It is not that the sum is thought to be greater than the size of its parts as in some formulations. It is rather that the system effects are *different* from its parts. We have seen how many notions in 'science', such as the properties of a gas, cannot be reduced to the subatomic particles whose seething movements constitute such a gas. As Kelly expresses this: 'Emergence requires a population of entities, a multitude, a collective. . . . More is different [since] . . . large numbers behave differently from small numbers' (1995: 26).

Moreover, with changes in the scientific theory and research, the basic individual constituents of the physical world have substantially shifted over time (from molecules, to atoms to subatomic particles). So there is simply no ultimately irreducible entity within science to which larger-scale properties have been universally reducible. Within quantum physics the apparent 'parts' consist of probabilistic *relationships* or patterns between sub-atomic particles, relationships that are not independent but are determined by the dynamics of the system as a whole. Heisenberg maintained that: 'The world thus appears as a complicated tissue of events, in which connections of different kinds alternate or overlap or combine and thereby determine the texture of the whole' (cited Capra 1996: 30).

'Rational action theorists' in the social sciences advocate redu-cing social patterns to various modes of individually rational, linear actions. But this seems wrong, since it presumes a clear and irreducible 'individual' whose rational actions can explain the social phenomena in question (see Goldthorpe 2000). There is no reason to presume that there are such clear and unambiguous rational individuals. Certainly the history of the physical sciences shows that there are no given and unchanging irreducible entities to which the complexity of the physical world has been, or could be, reduced. Indeed, what counts are the 'individual' results from multiple flows occurring over various times. According to De Landa (1997: 259–60), individual bodies and selves are mere 'transitory hardenings' in the more basic historical flows of min-erals, genes, diseases, energy, information, and language (see also chapter 2 above).

Emergent properties are also, as we have seen, never purely 'social' and the processes that generate them are also never simply social. Complexity would always argue against the thesis that 'phenomena' are bounded, that social causes produce social consequences, that there is a cause that generates linear effects. Causes are always overflowing, tipping from domain to domain and especially flowing across the supposedly distinct and puri-fied 'physical' and 'social' domains. For complexity, emergent properties are irreducible, interdependent, mobile and non-linear. Reductionism of the methodologically individualist sort is simply ruled out (although not in some complexity-influenced simulations). This chapter considers how to think through the nature of such irreducible, interdependent and mobile properties emergent at the *global* level. How it is that such global properties 'emerge', given that there would appear to be no single centre or 'governor' of the globe from which, in linear fashion, global relations can be derived?

It is instructive to begin with the best example of non-linear analysis within the social sciences – namely, Marx's analysis from a century and a half back of the unfolding 'contradictions' of the capitalist mode of production. He argued that the 'need for a constantly changing market chases the bourgeoisie over the whole surface of the globe. It must settle everywhere, establish connexions everywhere' (Marx and Engels 1848/1952: 46–7; see also Elster 1985; D. Harvey 2000). This putative globalization results from how individual capitalist enterprises seek to maximize profits and hence pay their workers as little as feasible or make them work as long as possible. This 'exploitation' of the workforce continues unless the state, or collective actions by trade unions, prevents it, or unless the workers die prematurely. The consequences of such endlessly repeated local actions reproduce the capitalist system and its emergent properties of class relations. Substantial profits are generated, so offsetting what Marx hypothesized as the tendency of the rate of profit to fall. Such profits reproduce the emergent class relations of capital and wage labour that are integral to the capitalist system. Out of those profits certain 'ideal collective interests' of capital are met through a 'capitalist state' that secures and sustains the legal form of private property, the availability of appropriate labour power, the conditions of the circulation of capital and so on.

However, Marx shows that sustaining order through each capitalist exploiting his or her *local* workforce eventually results in various system contradictions (see Elster 1985). First, since it is in the interests of each enterprise (but crucially not of all enterprises) to minimize the wages paid to its employees, the emergent level of demand for capitalist commodities is suboptimal (Elster 1985: 46–7). Hence, in relationship to demand there will be overproduction, the underemployment of capitalist resources (especially labour power) and periodic capitalist crises, although these are subsequently mitigated through 'Keynesian' policies that increase 'effective demand' for capitalist commodities.

Second, the effect of capitalist competition is to produce a workforce that is increasingly inefficient, relatively deprived and rebellious. Emergent from ordered capitalist relations is a working class that through an increasingly widespread class struggle will generate social revolution and ultimately the establishment of a 'higher' emergent order. In seeking its own transcendence from wage slavery, the proletariat generates a new communist order that overcomes the emergent contradictions of the capitalist system.

Third, the limitations of existing capitalist markets lead individual capitalist firms to seek alternative markets. *The Manifesto of the Communist Party* describes how the: 'need for a constantly changing market chases the bourgeoisie over the whole surface of the globe. It must settle everywhere, establish connexions everywhere . . . the bourgeoisie has through its exploitation of the world market given a cosmopolitan character to production and consumption in every country' (Marx and Engels 1848/1952: 46–7). This worldwide capitalist expansion will 'smash down Chinese walls' and ultimately generate the emergent property of a revolutionary proletariat stretching across the globe (Marx and Engels 1848/1952; D. Harvey 2000). Thus capitalist relations over millions of iterations result in the opposite of what capitalists appear to be reproducing through exploiting their *particular* workforce. Local capitalist exploitation results, Marx argues, in non-linear emergent effects of a revolutionary proletariat and a 'catastrophic' (in terms of the existing system) branching of capitalism into a new emergent order of world communism (see Reed and Harvey 1992).

We now know, through the benefits of hindsight, that his analysis was 'mistaken' in that it supposedly predicted worldwide social revolution. However, complexity can illuminate why. Complexity shows that relatively small perturbations in the capitalist system, such as the shift from an industrial to an informational paradigm (Castells 1996), would have produced a branching different from what was predicted by Marx a century and a half ago. Only a relatively small set of causes would have been necessary to generate a radically different emergent outcome, of post-Fordist 'welfare' consumerism rather than worldwide social revolution. Large effects do not necessarily need large causes, since systems out of equilibrium can tip or turn one way or the other through small rather than large changes.

Marx's analysis brings out the key significance both of local forms of information and action and of the emergence of system effects that are far from equilibrium. According to Marx, each capitalist firm operates under non-equilibrium conditions and is able to respond to 'local' sources of information that carries across a limited range. Any emergent complex system is then the result of a rich interaction of simple elements that 'only respond to the limited information each is presented with' (Cilliers 1998: 5; on the implications for social simulations, see also Gilbert 1995: 147–8). Thus, while across the world billions of actions occur, each is based upon localized information. People act iteratively in terms of what can be known locally and there is no global control over the system. Agents act in terms of the local environment but each agent adapts, or co-evolves, to local circumstances. But they adapt or co-evolve 'within an environment in which other similar agents are also adapting, so that changes in one agent may have consequences for the environment and thus the success of other agents' (Gilbert 1995: 148).

In the next section I suggest that, while people know little about the global connections or implications of their particular actions, these local actions nevertheless do not remain local. They are captured, represented, transported, marketed and generalized elsewhere. They get carried along the scapes and flows of the emerging global world, mobilizing ideas, people, images, moneys and technologies to potentially everywhere (rather like ping-pong balls in a gutter!). Examples were noted in previous chapters of where decisions based upon local knowledge have resulted through multiple iterations in unpredictable and non-linear consequences at the emergent global level. Thus the apparently 'rational' decision of millions of individual people to drive cars results in carbon gas emissions that threaten the planet's long-term survival. The Internet developed out of countless unplanned and relatively small-scale technological and organizational innovations occurring in a particular sequence. The almost overnight collapse of communism across Eastern Europe seems to have occurred once the particular local centre of the Kremlin was unable and unwilling to eliminate such rebellion.

Thus we might say that Marx's analysis of nineteenth-century capitalism demonstrates elements of complexity, although the 'emergent system' he analyses is demonstrably very different from that of today. Compared with the nineteenth-century system organized through the 'hegemon' of the British Empire, the current emergent order is structured through multiple inter-dependent organizations that are collectively performing the 'global'. Each co-evolves, demonstrating what Gilbert (1995: 151) terms a 'capability to "orientate" to macro-level properties', in this case at the global level.

These varied institutions include the UN (notably the Universal Declaration of Human Rights adopted on 10 December 1948), World Bank, Microsoft, World Trade Organization, Greenpeace, CNN, Inter-Governmental Committee on Climate Change, BBC, News Corporation, World Intellectual Property Organization, International Air Transport Association, FIFA, World Health Organization, IOC and so on (Held et al. 1999; UNDP 2000; Roche 2000). Through their *interdependence*, these institutions of governance and civil society are organizing the rules, structures and regulations of the newly emergent global order (on the contemporary interdependencies of the IOC, WHO, UN and so on, see Roche 2000). The nineteenth-century equivalent to this patterning was the 1884 establishment of Greenwich Mean Time that synchronized time zones across the world (Nguyen 1992: 33).

Interdependent with these global organizations are various signifiers of this emergent global order. Besides the blue earth, these include the Olympic Flag, the sea, Nelson Mandela, whales, tigers and elephants, the sign of the International Red Cross, the Amazon rain forest, Mother Teresa and so on. These signifiers reflect and perform a global imagined community uniting different peoples, genders and generations. The astronaut William Anders most famously commented on the image of the blue earth seen from space:

> The earth appeared as a small, blue-green sphere like a beautiful ornament, very delicate and limited. . . . The ancestral home of

mankind did not appear vast, unlimited and indestructible ...
Looking back, I saw no national boundaries, no dividing the earth
into separate states, each with a different colour as you see on a
globe in a schoolroom, a globe divided by man [*sic*] but obviously
not by nature' (cited in Menon 1997: 28; see also Cosgrove 1994)

Such images depict the globe through signifying certain iconic
places, peoples, environments and animals. And such images
also speak for the globe. Sklair (2001: 276–82) shows how very
many of the top 500 corporations use 'global imagery' in one
way or another in their branding and marketing for a global
marketplace.

Such organizations and images are fused together in various
planned, as well as unexpected, mega-events. On such occasions
the world views itself through such events placed upon the
world's mediatized public stage or screen. Examples include
World Expos, Live Aid concerts, Nelson Mandela's release from
prison, Rio Earth Summit, the terrorist destruction of the World
Trade Centre, Princess Diana's death and funeral, the Olympic
Games, millennial celebrations, World Cups, Beijing Women's
Conference and so on (Albrow 1996: 146; Roche 2000: ch. 7). In
each of these events global images are produced, circulated, recognized and consumed. The globe is produced and consumed on
screens around the world, especially through the spreading of
'ambient television' (McCarthy 2001).

Roche describes planned mega-events as 'social spatio-temporal
"hubs" and "switches" that ... channel, mix and re-route global
flows' (2000: 199). They are spatio-temporal moments of global
condensation, involving the peculiarly intense 'localization' of
such global events within 'unique places due to the fact that they
staged unique events', places that have the 'power to transform
themselves from being mundane places ... into being these
special "host city" sites' (Roche 2000: 224).

In the next section this relationship between global events and
local host cities is examined more generally. It is seen as a specific
illustration of a complexity analysis of the strange attractor of
'glocalization', whereby the connections of locally based actions
and global consequences have been so reconfigured since Marx's
brilliant insights from the middle of the century before last.

Strange Attractors

In Chapter 2 I discussed the idea of attractors and especially strange attractors. The latter characterize certain systems where spaces are unstable and to which the trajectory of dynamical systems is attracted over time through billions of iterations and processes of positive feedback.

There have been few attempts within the social sciences to develop analyses drawing on the notion of strange attractors (Byrne 1997, 1998). Baker's examination (1993: 135–41) of the 'centriphery' attractor is the most interesting (see also P. Stewart 2001: 331). Baker sees the centriphery as a dynamic pattern that gets repeated at many different levels of the social world. The centriphery involves irreversible flows of energy, information and ideas backwards and forwards between the centres and peripheries, with each existing only because of the other. And the centriphery simultaneously creates and re-creates both centres *and* peripheries. The trajectory of social systems is irreversibly attracted to this centriphery attractor. Because centring and peripheralizing involve the transformation of energy and information and, thus, the creation of entropy, the process is irreversible.

> Centering, then is an 'attractor', creating order by funnelling energy and information towards itself and disorder by peripheralizing its environment. It produces a world on the periphery where the flow of energy and information is away to somewhere else . . . the center has an entropic effect on the periphery, causing increased randomness and increasing amounts of unusable resources. (Baker 1993: 139)

The centriphery is rather like Einstein's conception of an object whose gravity warps the space around it, drawing in and generating new patterns of order *and* of disorder. And further, Baker notes that such centring processes are now significantly internationalized. Thus: 'today, particular multinational industries center vast amounts of human activity, locating specific aspects of their enterprise in different continents. In each of these cases, the exchange of goods and services binds and lubricates a dynamic relationship between the center and the periphery. As centering progresses, it deepens the periphery' (Baker 1993: 140).

Baker's account is now historically dated, since it depends upon the relatively simple thesis of the internationalizing of industrial production. However, his argument can be developed through suggesting that the specific form now taken by the attractor of the centriphery is 'glocalization'. Within the phase-space of various possibilities, the trajectories of many social systems worldwide are increasingly drawn into the attractor of 'glocalization' (on the 'glocal', see Robertson 1992). By this I mean that there are parallel, irreversible and mutually interdependent processes by which globalization-deepens-localization-deepens-globalization and so on. The global and the local are inextricably and irreversibly bound together through a dynamic relationship, with huge flows of 'resources' moving backwards and forwards between the two. Neither the global nor the local exists without the other. The global–local develops in a symbiotic, unstable and irreversible set of relationships, in which each gets transformed through billions of worldwide iterations dynamically evolving over time.

What has produced such attractor effects? Crucial to Marx's account of the contradictions of nineteenth-century capitalism was its foundation upon the localized nature of information. Each firm responds only to locally available information. And more generally this system of localized informational limitation more or less remained in place until the late twentieth century (Cilliers 1998: 4). The radio, TV, letter, telegram and fixed line telephone enabled some input of information from outside each locality. Heidegger wrote about the first in 1919: 'I live in a dull, drab colliery village . . . a bus ride from third rate entertainments and a considerable journey from any educational, musical or social advantages of a first class sort. . . . Into this monotony comes a good radio set and my little world is transformed' (cited in Scannell 1996: 161). The radio (and later the TV) began to disclose the public world of events, persons and happenings. People were partially thrown into the public world disclosed on radio and TV.

But my claim here is that the scale, range of media and extensivity of informational flows developing from around 1990 have irreversibly transformed such 'disclosures' from elsewhere. Information flows have been dematerialized from place. With digitization, information adopts patterns and modes of mobility substantially separate from material form or presence. Information gets everywhere (and nowhere) travelling more or less instantaneously along the fluid networks of global communications, along what was referred to in chapter 4 as 'all-channel' networks.

These technologies change at astonishing speed, with a hundredfold increase in computing power every ten years (Brand 1999). The new 'computime' represents the abstraction of time and its separation from human experience, space and the rhythms of nature. The information-based digital age 'is about the global movement of weightless bits at the speed of light' (Negroponte 1995: 12). What can be accessed locally or globally is now more or less identical, or at least is irreversibly becoming identical (see Cairncross 1998). And it is this spatial indifference of information that has called into being the strange attractor of glocalization. This involves the remaking of social relations across the world, as extraordinarily diverse social practices get irreversibly 'drawn into' or 'sucked into' the ambit of the glocalizing attractor.

A number of almost simultaneous, and partly contingent, transformations occurred from around 1990 to 'kick-start' this dynamically different informational order (see Castells 1996). First, Soviet Communism collapsed. The societies of Central and Eastern Europe had constructed exceptionally strong frontiers both from the 'West' and from each other. The cold war chilled information and culture as well as politics. But from 1989 the system disappeared almost overnight, partly because of the profound failure of Soviet Communism to develop new informational technologies and the paradoxical dependence upon US computing technology (see Castells 1998: ch. 1). And, as it disappeared, especially following the mega-event of the demolition of the Berlin Wall, so substantial localized barriers to informational flow also dissolved.

Simultaneously, there was the development of systems of global news reporting, as opposed to the national news reporting that impressed Heidegger in the 1920s. CNN television started in 1980, but, since its 'success' in the Gulf War, broadcasts in over 140 countries. This more or less virtual war in 1991 was the first in which the new pattern of twenty-four-hour real-time reporting occurred across the world. This greatly increased CNN's visibility and this has subsequently spread to many other broadcasters that have gone global and produced a 'global stage/screen' for many events now thoroughly mediated (Volkmer 1999; Hoskins 2001).

Analogously in the late 1980s all major financial markets moved to on-line real-time trading accessible somewhere or other twenty-four hours a day. There was a shift to a global system of electronic financial trading (Leyshon and Thrift 1997).

But, most telling, in 1990 Tim Berners-Lee 'invented' the World Wide Web and especially the concepts of URL, HTTP and HTML (see Castells's history: 2001). Together these concepts enable seamless jumps from link to link without regard to the conventional geographical boundaries within which information had been located, stored and curated (Friedman 2000: 65–6). Also developing from around 1990 was a cascading array of books, articles, web sites and symposia devoted to examining this new global ordering. These analyses both detail the strong co-evolution of informational flows occurring across the globe within very different domains of activity; and assist in citing, performing and drawing into existence a new global ordering always balanced on the knife edge, 'on the edge of chaos'.

My argument here is that there is not a global centre of power, let alone a global conspiracy or global networks unattached to social practice (see the critique in Jessop 2000). Rather there is an attractor of 'glocalization'. This is developing on a progressively worldwide basis and drawing more and more sets of relationships into its awesome power. And, as relationships are drawn in, so they are irreversibly remade. This is productive of a new ordering but not one involving a single coordinating centre. Kwa describes this notion as 'complexity without telos. . . . Any local change, provided it meets the critical requirements, can induce the rest of the population . . . to "co-operate" into finding a new mode of behaviour. All individuals seem to be informed about each other at the steps of the transition' (2002: 42; see also Duffield 2001).

One illustration of the workings of this attractor is how global mega-events such as the Olympics seem both to presuppose the emergence of local host cities and to reinforce their emergence. These are places chosen for their supposedly unique, *local* characteristics that make them especially appropriate for the hosting of what are increasingly *global* events (Roche 2000). More generally, the recent period has seen the development of a global *screen* upon which localities, cultures and nations appear, to compete and to mobilize themselves as spectacle (P. Harvey 1996; Roche 2000). These events, premised upon global media and mass tourism, mean that local identity and nation are conceived of through their location within, and upon, that global screening.

This 'global screening' in turn relates to the changing nature of nationality (Maier 1994: 149–50; McCrone 1998). Once nationality was based upon a homogenous and mapped national territory, in which law was defined, authority claimed and loyalty sought by the state within that territory. But now frontiers are permeable and cultural life is far more interchangeable across the globe through extensive corporeal, imaginative and virtual travel. Maier concludes that 'territory is less central to national self-definition' (1994: 149). Nationality gets more constituted through specific *local* places, symbols and landscapes, icons of the nation central to that culture's location within the contours of global business, travel and branding (such as the twin towers of New York's World Trade Centre).

Through glocalization, then, nation has become less a matter of the specific state uniquely determining that nation. And the notion of nation has significantly become more a matter of branding, as nation has become something of a free-floating signifier relatively detached from the 'state' within the swirling contours of the new global order (see P. Harvey 1996; Delanty 2000: 94). British PM Tony Blair famously talked of seeking to 'rebrand Britain'.

The power of the attractor of glocalization can also be seen in the more general development of global brands *and* of the often localized resistances that develop against them. I noted in the last chapter the insidious power of such brands, a virus sent out into the culture through various channels of sponsorship, consumerism, political controversy and marketing additions. Brands are, moreover, always on the move, often ironically flowing in and out of cultures, including cultures of protest. Brands do not just seep downwards from the centre – they also derive from various street life and cultures, turning almost every local resistance into a rebranding opportunity (such as urban black youth, New Age, feminism, labour movement, Greens and so on).

Simultaneously there is a growing global opposition to the 'branded life'. Brands create their opposite via the parodying of advertisements (Cancer Country rather than Marlboro County cigarettes), through local and then global 'reclaiming of the street' parties, through Critical Mass bike rides, through the international anti-sweatshops movement (especially targeting Nike, Gap, Wal-Mart, Disney and so on for their localized labour market exploitation) and through massive NGO campaigns against Shell, McDonalds and 'globalization' more generally (Klein 2000: 309). Klein (2000: 441) shows how the attractor works:

> by trying to enclose our shared culture in sanitized and controlled brand cocoons, these corporations have themselves created the surge of opposition . . . they have radicalized that opposition. . . . By abandoning their traditional role as direct, secure employers to pursue their branding dreams, they have lost the loyalty that once protected them from citizen rage.

More generally, given the conflictual and antagonistic relations between globalization and localization, the global 'always confronts forms of resistance and structural limits that make a fully constituted globality hard to imagine' (Jessop 2000: 357). A banner at a global street party pointedly read: 'The resistance will be as transnational as capital', while an organizer of such a party ironically talks of the 'United Colours of Resistance' (Klein 2000: 322, 357).

More generally, passionate opposition to the networks and flows of the new global order energizes many networked groups and associations. Globalization generates its opposition, forming an 'elaborate web' that especially opposes 'McGovernment' (Klein 2001: 86). Such a resistant order to global institutions is fragmented and disparate, including the Zapatistas in Mexico, the American Militia and the Patriots more generally, Aum Shinrikyo in Japan, global terrorists, many environmental NGOs, the women's movement concerned with the impacts of the global marketplace upon women and children in developing countries, New Ageists, religious fundamentalist movements, the Global Resistance movement and so on. All oppose aspects of the new global ordering and are organized through 'resistance identities' (Castells 1997: 356).

These are virtual communities that 'exist only to the extent that their constituents are linked together through identifications constructed in the non-geographic spaces of activist discourses, cultural products and media images' (Rose 1996: 333). And, partly through their practices of resistance to the flows, they serve to 'detotalize' and 'localize' each national society. Thus 'civil societies shrink and disarticulate because there is no longer continuity between the logic of power-making in the global network [global fluids, in my terminology here] and the logic of association and representation in specific societies and cultures' (Castells 1997: 11).

Paradoxically, such groups routinely employ the machines and technologies of globalization. Castells (1997: ch. 3) terms the Zapatistas the 'first informational guerrillas', since they deploy computer mediated communication and the establishment of a global electronic network of solidarity groups. Similar widespread use of the Internet is found amongst the American Patriots, who believe that the federal state is turning the USA into a part of the global economy and destroying American sovereignty and local customs and culture. And the Internet has been central to those planning the massive protests against the key symbols of the new global order, the World Trade Organization and the meetings of the G7/G8. Organizations like the WTO also came under attack in cyberspace, as worldwide direct action used the Internet to jam their computer system and to broadcast information on the unfolding event.

Deterritorialized global entities are strikingly vulnerable to the processes of democratic 'mobilization' by similarly mobile, deterritorialized social movements of a fused private-in-public. On public screens across the world the images of peaceful protestors being beaten over the head by American police are globally circulated. The WTO has been unable to force through the new round of trade liberalization. It was subject to public shaming via global screening that exposed the economic private realm to a global public (see Sheller and Urry 2002). Moreover, this event was only one of many in a wave of protest reverberating around the world and its screens with similar 'anti-capitalist' events springing up in June 1999, May Day 2000, July 2001 and so on. As the organizers put it, 'Our resistance is as global as capital' (see http://www.freespeech.org/mayday2k).

Thus new 'organizations' have developed that are globally mediated. People imagine themselves as members (or supporters) of such organizations through purchases, wearing the T-shirt, hearing the CD, surfing the organization's page on the Web, participating in a computerized jamming and so on. However, for all the power of global fluids, 'members' of organizations will intermittently come together to 'be with' others in the present, in moments of intensely *localized* fellow-feeling. These moments, involving what has been called the 'compulsion to proximity', include festivals, business conferences, holidays, camps, training camps for terrorists, seminars and, of course, sites of global protest (Boden and Molotch 1994; Szerszynski 1997; Urry 2002b).

The workings of the glocalization attractor can also be seen in global financial systems. Such systems have got progressively disembedded from place with the commodification of markets operating through twenty-four-hour global trading in real time. But this global disembedding occurs only with a simultaneous intensification of the 'local'. Because of the fragile and symbolic communities that are formed in electronic money space, so re-embedded particularistic spaces develop to cement relationships of trust more intensely. New meeting places become nodes of reflexivity that then resonate back over billions of iterations across time to enhance and augment the globally organized electronic money spaces.

Boden summarizes how the attractor operates:

> Surrounded by complex technology and variable degrees of uncertainty, social actors seek each other out, to make the deals that, writ large across the global electronic boards of the exchanges, make the market. They come together in tight social worlds to use each other and their shared understanding of 'what's happening' to reach out and move those levers that move the world. (Boden 2000: 194)

New places of face-to-face interaction have sprung up in the City of London, so stabilizing the informational frenzy of twenty-four-hour global trading. There is an increased importance of the business lunch (less drink and meat-based with 'feminization'), the conference, residential training, corporate hospitality and even the business card (Leyshon and Thrift 1997: 349–50). Financial practices across almost all countries are drawn into and are organized through such relations between locally tight social worlds of intense trust, on the one hand, and hugely disembedded and abstracted global money space, on the other. Each strengthens and reinforces the other, as many other trading patterns get drawn into, and transformed through, such a glocalized attractor.

Something similar seems to characterize work relations in the software industry. Ó Riain (2000) describes how software developers rely upon intense 'team' working in order to offset two features of their global experience. First, the workforce, in this case involved in software development in Ireland, is multicultural, so forms of face-to-face bonding are necessary to deal with an otherwise disruptive 'difference'. And, second, these developers have very mobile careers and relatively fleeting associations with each other. So what is required is 'an intense experience of a shared space and culture in order to create a cohesive work team' (Ó Riain 2000: 189). These places 'are increasingly "between" other places' and are part of the 'innovative regional milieu' that is to be found in and around Dublin (Ó Riain 2000: 189).

A somewhat broader account of glocalization can be seen in Thomas Friedman's *The Lexus and the Olive Tree* (2000). Half the world he says is intent on producing a better Lexus through modernizing, streamlining and privatizing their economies so as to thrive within a global world. This is the 'first modernity'. And the other half is caught up in a fight to determine who owns which olive tree, the olive tree standing for roots, anchoring, identity, what Lash (1999) calls 'another modernity'. Olive trees also involve excluding others. So the struggle between the Lexus and the olive tree is taken by Friedman as a metaphor for the kinds of relationships that characterize the new global order. They are not always in conflict – consider the Global Positioning System (GPS) to enable Muslim air passengers to know exactly where the plane is in relationship to Mecca.

Barber (1996) sees the glocal attractor in apocalyptic terms. He describes the emergent global order as increasingly locked into a conflict between consumerist 'McWorld', on the one hand, and the identity politics of the 'Jihad', on the other. There is a 'new world disorder' in which McWorld and Jihad depend upon, and globally reinforce, each other. Together they constitute a strange attractor, a spiralling global disequilibrium that threatens existing public spheres, civil society and democratic forms. He argues that 'the dialectical interaction between them suggest new and startling forms of inadvertent tyranny that range from an invisibly constraining consumerism to an all too palpable barbarism' (Barber 1996: 220).

Such a strange attractor moreover involves existing nationally encoded notions of 'citizenship' being drawn into two alternatives, of consumerism, on the one hand, and localist identity politics, on the other. Thus existing nationally focused notions of citizenship are drawn into and transformed through the strange attractor of 'glocalization'. All sorts of further relations get drawn into a gravity effect of such an attractor. Islam, Hinduism, 'born-again' Christianity and many 'local' religions themselves come to develop global characteristics, each seemingly knowledgeable about how each is developing a global visibility and responding to such processes of co-evolution (see Appadurai 1996).

Finally, post-Communist Hungary illuminates how the attractor of glocalization can be said to draw diverse sets of relations into its powerful embrace (Gille 2000). Eastern Europe is typically now viewed as a wasteland – of the failed political project of Communism and of an economy that generated disproportionate amounts of waste. The siting of a new waste incinerator plant in Garé on the site of a waste dump funded in part by the EU relates both to the nature of the global waste incineration industry and to the global environmental movement. The EU is funding the building of various waste incinerator plants in former Eastern Europe, plants that would turn local waste into energy. However, according to the greens such sites would also incinerate West European waste, out of sight and smell of West Europeans. So the siting of a waste incinerator plant in Garé appears to be the product of 'globalization', aided and abetted by the EU, and explicable in terms of the logic of the global waste incineration industry.

However, Gille presents an analysis more consistent with the thesis of a powerful glocalization attractor. Thus one effect of complex post-Communist politics within Hungary has been the relative disappearance of the national state. This enabled this specific locality of Garé to form a direct relationship with the company originally responsible for the waste dump in order to get an incinerator built on the site. Relationships were established with various other global companies, while EU funding was also secured. Local elites in favour of the incinerator were able to mobilize a strong sense of local history, which helped to sustain objections to neighbouring localities and to global 'greens' seeking to influence outcomes from outside. Gille summarizes the global–local relationships operating here: 'The void created by the state's disappearance from Garé's life . . . was quickly filled by global forces and discourses that the new [local] elite success-fully utilized in its own interests. . . . Such a direct connection between local and global could not have emerged under social-ism, as the state's umbrella shielded localities from global weath-ers, rain or shine' (2000: 252). She thus summarizes how 'global forces . . . are less constraining and more enabling than they once were' as society after society is drawn into and remade through what is termed, in this book, the glocalizing attractor (Gille 2000: 261).

Global Emergence

So far I have shown that there is no global society or single centre of global power and hence no clear-cut global 'region'. There is also no unambiguous set of outcomes providing evidence of the power of 'global' processes. I thus argue against those who main-tain that globalization produces a set of linear effects, such as the heightened homogenization of culture, or increased socio-economic inequalities, or the worldwide growth of democracies.

What is treated here as the 'global' produces no single set of effects, although it is bound up with all those processes just men-tioned. The development of the attractor of glocalization entails a wholesale shifting in the very structure of economic, social and political relations across the globe. However, the evidence for this does not consist of a set of effects that can provide a direct 'test' or 'measurement' of the 'global'. Of course, there must be sub-stantial programmes of research examining these sets of putatively 'global' relations.

According to Abbott (2001: ch. 1), much social science assumes a 'linear reality' in which the social world consists of fixed entities with variable attributes, that these attributes have only one meaning, that the past sequencing of events is irrelevant and that context does not affect these attributes. He makes a general argument against such a position, but global processes and especially the global–local processes that construct and reconstruct the *relations* between the global and local further undermine the notion that there are or indeed could be clear and unambiguous fixed entities with variable properties whose history is irrelevant. Indeed the 'evidence' that relationships across the globe are being globalized is necessarily ambivalent, contradictory and contestable. If it is right to argue for a complexity formulation of the emerging system, then the research needs to reflect and capture uneven, far-from-equilibrium sets of interdependent processes involved in the very making of the global and especially of the glocalizing attractor (as Duffield (2001) argues for global governance).

Held et al. (1999: 17) do provide massive evidence of an extensivity of global networks and flows, an intensity of interconnectedness, a velocity of mobilities around the globe and the high impact of such interconnectedness. And these have powerful effects, especially of powerful local perturbations in the system that result in unpredictable branching emerging across the global system. Examples of these local perturbations include the demolition of the Berlin Wall, the invention of the first Web browser in the USA, the release from a South African prison of Nelson Mandela, and the presence of twenty bombers on four American planes on 11 September 2001.

But such emergent effects are often produced by 'small causes' and these get relayed through the diverse and overlapping global networks and fluids that interact physically, and especially informationally, under, over and across the earth's surface, stretching over hugely different temporal scales. These interactions are rich, non-linear and move towards the attractor of 'glocalization'. There is no simple empirical research here of unambiguous global or local entities. Rather, the processes are much more like 'gravity'. There is an increasingly powerful gravity effect upon numerous, diverse localized patterns. Such globally complex systems, especially developing from around 1990 and the desubstantiation of information, involve positive feedback loops that render the global far from equilibrium as many entities are drawn into the attractor relationships.

Further, this set of global systems is like no other social system. Its emergent features make it different from anything that has gone before. Paradoxically it does have some similarities with feudal Europe. Some have described the globalizing world as 'neo-feudal'. In the global world there are *multiple* political units beyond individual societies (see Walby 2001); there are *empires*, such as Coca-Cola, Microsoft or Disney, more powerful than societies (see Klein 2000); there are competing *city states*, such as London, Sydney or Los Angeles (see Roche 2000); and there are many *wandering intellectuals, sports stars, musicians and so on*, as well as international *vagrants*, with declining national attachments (see Urry 2002a). But there are also many differences between emergent global ordering and European feudalism, especially in terms of the technologies of the household and of warfare, production, circulation, distribution, and exchange, such that few useful lessons can be drawn from such a comparison.

Likewise the system of nation states seems to bear few resemblances to global systems. The former is organized through a nation state that 'governs' its citizens, there are clear boundaries and memberships, they possess a self-organizing character, and each derives a unity from opposition to each 'other'. There is a *system* of competing, self-organizing nation states that characterized the twentieth century (albeit with plenty of exceptions). Global systems, by contrast, are not governed by a central state, although there are very significant attempts by the corporate world to draw up various rules for global governance in their interests. Monbiot rather brilliantly describes the 'corporate bid for world domination' (2000: ch. 10).

Thus we are confronted with a global social laboratory but one within which we have almost no guides to appropriate investigation. Three things are sure. Developments towards the global are irreversible but unpredictable. The global possesses systemic characteristics that urgently demand investigation and are distinct from those of other social systems. And, since the global is like nothing else, the social sciences have to start more or less from scratch. Existing theories such as that of class domination will not work when converted onto the global level. Hence there are significant limitations of Sklair's hugely ambitious efforts (2001) to write class theories as global.

Complexity has thus been drawn on here, since it deals with odd and unpredictable systems often far from equilibrium and without a central 'governor'. Complexity we have seen emphasizes that no distinctions should be drawn between structure and process, stability and change, and a system and its environment (see Duffield's analogous formulation from security studies: 2001).

I have resisted defining 'globalization' as a single, clear and unambiguous 'causal' entity. Jessop similarly argues that globalization is 'best interpreted as the complex resultant of many different processes rather than as a distinctive causal process in its own right' (2000: 339). If we resist distinguishing between structure and process, stability and change, a system and its environment, then there is indeed no 'globalization' as a causal entity involved in 'contests' with various other regions. There are in more formal language no such entities with variable attributes (Abbott 2001). There are 'many different processes', but the key question is how they are organized within certain emergent irreversible global outcomes that move backwards and forwards between the more localized and more global levels. On such an account then globalization is a characterization of the system as 'effect' rather than as in any sense a 'cause', although I have noted the likely inappropriateness of such causal language (Rosenberg 2000). This leads me to thinking the global through the lens of performativity. I will now consider such a way of thinking the global.

First, the 'globe' is an object of concern for many citizens across many different countries. I noted above the remarkably widespread availability of *global* images, in TV programmes, branding by global corporations, adverts and especially political campaigns. Also countless oppositional organizations concerned with aspects of global governance have developed since the 1960s. There are also many more formal organizations, especially since the founding of the UN in 1948, that take the whole earth as an object of reflexive concern. The globe has become an object of widespread reflexivity stretching across the world in the face of what has been termed the 'world risk society' (Beck 1998). With such a development we can experience at least putatively the 'end of the other'.

Modern science has created this monster of the global risk society through treating the environment as its laboratory. But science has also

> demonstrated that the Earth is a lonely fragile spaceship that is the only home for all humanity, however riven by divisions based on nationality, religion, colour, community or ethnicity; how it has made the world a small place with the capabilities now available for movement of ideas, information, people, goods and services; and how it has demonstrated the fundamental and essential oneness of all living systems. (Menon 1997: 35–6)

Nobel prizewinner Joseph Rotblat argues that we can and must develop an allegiance to 'humanity' rather than to the 'nation' (1997a: pp. x–xi). It is global *interdependence* between the world's population that is the key to developing a universalist allegiance to 'humanity' rather than to national identities. He maintains that:

> The fantastic progress in communication and transportation has transformed the world into an intimately interconnected community, in which all members depend on one another for their well-being. We are now able to observe instantly what is going on in any part of the globe and provide help where necessary. . . . We must exploit the many new channels of communication to bring us together and form a truly global community. We must become world citizens. (Rotblat 1997a: pp. x–xi; see also Walby 2001)

The Pugwash Conference on Science and World Affairs expects and indeed hopes that the global media will play a particularly significant role in this but not only because they carry cognitive information across the globe. Rather, cultural work is carried through co-present media *images* that are able to engender 'an emotional response to the world events that they portray'; such images heighten the awareness of regional and global interdependence and put pressure on offending governments to moderate their often offensive actions (Rotblat 1997a: 14). More generally, Vaclav Havel describes how the 'perspective of a better future depends on something like an international community of citizens

. . . standing outside the high game of traditional politics . . . will seek to make a real political force out of . . . the phenomenon of human conscience' (cited Rapoport 1997: 97; on 'distant others', see also S. Cohen 2001).

Furthermore, scientists (and other groups of professionals) are increasingly organized in a post-national manner. They are almost 'quasi-nations', with their own system of globally organized events, timetables and rewards (such as Nobel and other prizes). And, as modern electronic communications develop, so these quasi-nations become more important, widespread and drawn into the attractor of glocalization. Professionals indeed see the global village as replacing the nation state, as electronic communication supplants written communication and the 'whole earth' replaces the 'territory with borders'. There is a widespread sense of the increasing role that communities that cut across national boundaries play in the lives of ordinary people (Rotblat 1997b). Various authorities have talked of the growth of a 'transnational civil society as an arena for struggle' (Keck and Sikkink 1998: 33), as well as massively extensive and self-organizing 'ungrounded empires' like the overseas Chinese (Ong and Nonini 1997).

Some analysts also argue that women are more likely to be drawn to notions of global citizenship. Women appear to be more opposed to wars (on the Gulf War, see Shaw 1994: 127). They often find the maleness of symbols of national power particularly alienating (Yuval-Davis 1997). Survey evidence shows that they are particularly committed to conservation and environmental issues (Anderson 1997: 174). Thus women are more likely to convince others of the superiority of a relatively countryless notion of citizenship and indeed to advance a notion of universal rights under which specific women's rights, such as freedom from sexual violence, can be lodged (Shiva 1989; Kaplan 1996; Walby 2001).

So various social practices, of science, the media, international groupings, women and so on, which stem from the putative universalism of the globe as an object of reflexive concern, may begin to make or perform the global. *Global Nature, Global Culture* formulates a conception of the global as 'performance' (Franklin et al. 2000). Indeed, it uses various complexity notions: of ideas of catastrophe, chaos and fractals, of how global culture is partially self-organizing, of the open character of the global system, of the importance of iteration and of the generally disruptive effects of specific informational flows. There is a strong recognition of the complex, non-linear and temporally irreversible character of global processes.

The authors draw especially on Butler's claim that performativity 'must be understood not as a singular or deliberative "act", but rather, as the reiterative and citational practice by which discourse produces the effects that it names' (1993: 2). Butler brings out the crucial importance of iteration for performance. Structures are never fixed or given for good. They always have to be worked at over time. And naming something (such as the global) is itself partly to call that which is named into being. Franklin, Lury and Stacey argue that the global is 'performed' by itself and is not caused by something outside itself, not does it cause effects external to it. The global is seen as auto-enabled or auto-reproduced, although they do not use the term 'autopoeisis' from complexity (see chapter 2 above). Thus they examine how the global is being brought into being as an emergent effect, as it comes to constitute its own domain especially through various material-semiotic practices (Franklin et al. 2000: 5). The global is shown to be 'performed, imagined and practised' across numerous domains that are operating at enormously different scales or levels.

The authors also describe how the global 'enters' the self through what they portray as the 'intimate global'. Because of the shift from 'kind' to 'brand', they describe how nature is being drawn into the attractor of globalization. Nature gets commodified, technologized, reanimated and rebranded. And many material-semiotic practices – from the economic, to politics, to medical science, to theme parks, to computer technology – are involved in the global remaking of culture and nature and especially the increasing fusion of the two.

Does this therefore mean that we should conceive of the global system as autopoietic (see chapter 2 above)? Is the global system self-making? Maturana writes how autopoietic systems 'are defined as networks of productions of components that recursively, through their interactions, generate and realize the network that produces them and constitute, in the space in which they exist, the boundaries of the network as components that participate in the realization of the network' (1981: 21). Such a system is thus not a set of relations between static components with fixed attributes. Rather there are processes of self-making through iteration over time of the production of components that are in fact necessary to make up that very system. There is continuous regeneration of the processes of production through an array of feedback mechanisms (Capra 1996: 168).

In a sociological context Luhmann has most deployed this notion of autopoiesis. He defines it thus: 'everything that is used as a unit by the system is produced as a unit by the system itself. This applies to elements, processes, boundaries, and other structures and, last but not least, to the unity of the system itself' (Luhmann 1990: 3; see also Mingers 1995). Such systems deploy 'communications' as the 'particular mode of autopoietic reproduction', since only communications are necessarily social. A theory of autopoietic systems involves the development of communications as the elementary component of each system. Such communications are not living or conscious units but involve three elements, information, utterance and understanding. Luhmann understands these as co-created within the processes of communication. Social systems are not 'closed systems' but open systems that are recursively closed with respect to such communications. Such communications result, he says, in the self-making of 'our well-known society' (Luhmann 1990: 13; see also P. Stewart 2001). These systems increase their complexity and their selectivity in order to reduce the complexity of the environment in which they have to operate (Luhmann 1990: 84).

How relevant is autopoiesis to examining the nature of *global systems*? Certainly, the notion of autopoiesis bears some similarities with analyses in *Global Nature, Global Culture* as to the spreading of global communications and consequential remaking of the natural and cultural domains around the world. Autopoiesis also bears a resemblance to the argument that it is through naming the global, and through billions of iterations, that the global is then brought into being. Luhmann talks of the differentiations involved in the development of 'world society'.

However, Luhmann's argument is couched at too high a level of abstraction to grasp the very specific character of the global networks and fluids that I outlined and defended above (for a more circumscribed application, see Medd 2000). Luhmann's account is functionalist, not capturing the contingent, far-from-equlibrium processes implicated in the current world 'on the edge of chaos'. Feedbacks are predominantly negative rather than positive. Luhmann refers to 'our well-known society'. But this suggests that the general concept of self-making cannot be connected to the very detailed workings of networked phenomena that are complex, fractured entities often operating far from equilibrium. These limitations are even more problematic where such notions of self-making weakly capture the extensivity of global networks and flows, the intensity of global interconnectedness, the heightened velocity of mobilities around the globe and the massive impact of such interconnectedness.

Indeed, applying Luhmann's autopoeitic formulation to the global or 'world society' would result in a 'global functionalism' where everything that affects the system across the globe is seen as contributing to its self-making. Thus the massive inequalities that accompany globalization, or the rising of global temperatures through 'global warming', or the growth of global terrorism might all be viewed as necessary functional components of the processes of global self-making. This position is unconvincing. But so too is an alternative view that treats the global as the clear and determinant outcome of a partially self-conscious transnational capitalist class (Sklair 2001).

Conclusion

Thus the notion of global self-making seems plausible, but *the* global system as a whole should not be viewed as autopoeitic. How to combine these positions here?

It is necessary here to return to the discussion of Prigogine developed in chapter 2. He shows how new pockets of order arise that are often far from equilibrium. These pockets involve dissipative structures, islands of new order within a general sea of disorder. He argues that these islands of order can maintain or even increase their order at the expense of greater overall entropy or disorder. Prigogine describes how each of these pockets of order 'floats in disorder' (see Capra 1996: 184). It is various contexts well away from equilibrium that are sources of such new localized order. Examples of such pockets of order are turbulent flows of water and air that appear chaotic but that are in fact highly organized. Such turbulent flows involve processes of self-making with highly effective feedback mechanisms.

It seems that Prigogine's formulation provides an important key to understanding global complexity. This position will be briefly summarized, since it provides the basis for the revived social science of the global developed in the next chapter.

First then, contrary to the claims of a number of authorities, there is no single equilibrating global system (see Sklair 2001). There is also no 'other' to the global that, as with other social systems, is necessary for governmentality and social order.

But there are systematic forms of global interdependence or what is termed here global complexity. This 'system' is hugely open, comprising various interdependent and hybridized networks and fluids. They move in, through and across time–space, in remarkably different and contrasting trajectories. There is no tendency of this global 'system' to move towards any obvious equilibrium. And there is no evidence that this global system is *in toto* organized through autopoeitic self-making, in part because it would be impossible to specify what the relationships are between the array of biological, social and physical processes involved in such a system *and* its environment. We should avoid positing a global functionalism or a global conspiracy, especially in the light of the critiques of both formulations developed over the past century.

However, global complexity is not simply anarchic disorder. There are many pockets of ordering within this overall patterning of disorder, processes involving a particular performing of the global and operating over multiple time–space with various feedback processes. Such pockets of ordering include various networks, fluids and governance mechanisms. These different pockets of order develop *parallel* concepts and processes of what we call the global. At different levels there are what we may term 'global fractals', the irregular but strangely similar shapes that are found at very different scales across the world, from the household say to the UN.

And, as such pockets of ordering emerge, so various often very substantial non-linear effects of 'global–local' objects, identities, institutions and social practices develop. These come to form and to elaborate the strange attractor of glocalization. Like gravity, this attractor can be viewed as drawing multiple sets of social relationships worldwide into its tender embrace and restructuring such relationships through countless iterations that occur over substantial periods of time. The speed, range and depth of especially the informational and transport revolutions heighten the interdependent non-linear effects of such glocalizing relationships across the world.

Thus there are pockets of order (or ordering) within a sea of global disorder. And, indeed, such pockets of ordering operating at different time–space scales heighten the turbulence, the risk cultures, of the global sea of disorder, as I elaborate in the following chapter.

6

Social Ordering and Power

Social Order and Global Complexity

A long-standing issue in sociology and social science more generally concerns how some kind of order gets established and maintained in social life. Early formulations, such as Herbert Spencer's, maintained that the workings of the social body were analogous to those of the human body. And, as societies develop and grow, there is, as with the body, an increase in the structural differentiation of specialized functions. The social body, like the human body, is characterized by the interdependence and integration of the separate parts. Explaining any particular social institution is achieved by showing its contribution or 'function' to the reproduction of the social organism as a whole (Spencer 1876/1893).

Talcott Parsons (1960) generally argued that *the* central issue for sociology is how it is that social order is secured and sustained. In order to answer this he developed a *normative* functionalist analysis. Order in societies gets maintained through normative consensus rather than through either the interdependencies of the marketplace, as Spencer argued, or the coercive relations of economic, political and ideological domination, as Marx and others maintained.

However, for a number of reasons, these and other formulations from 'classical sociology' now seem very dated. First, these sociologists did not distinguish between a living *organism* and a living *system*. They concentrated upon the characteristics of the former in order to derive appropriate metaphors for understanding how order within a social system is possible. They did not see how the properties of living *systems* might provide appropriate analysis of social order, given that order is never simple, fixed and achieved. The science of complex systems provides a way of thinking about social order that transcends the static nature of classical sociological functionalism, where the fixed parts of the social body are seen as providing specific functions within the workings of the social whole.

Second, classical sociology tended to adopt a relatively simple notion of what constitutes 'social order'. In Parsons there is a hierarchy of values and norms that works through each society at all levels, a clear notion of social equilibrium, and strong negative feedback or steering mechanisms that can rapidly and effectively restore order. But the implications of complexity, as opposed to the early post-Second World War cybernetics that influenced Parsons, is that there never is such a clear and effective set of re-equilibriating processes. And, indeed, efforts to restore social order almost always engender further unforeseen consequences. These are often of a kind that take the society further away from any ordered equilibrium. In a later section of this chapter I consider the extraordinarily 'complex' and unpredictable character of 'mediatized scandals' as an example of the systemic workings of such unforeseen consequences. The classical tradition little considered the mobile patterning of social life that problematizes the fixed, given and static notions of social order. Ordering one might say is achieved 'on the move'.

Third, formulations from classical and early twentieth-century sociology deploy a society focus with little recognition of how what lies beyond each society's borders is relevant to apparent social ordering (Urry 2000b: ch. 1). For Parsons, such a notion of autonomous self-reproducing societies stemmed from the apparent autonomy of American society throughout the twentieth century. He then universalized this characteristic to all other apparent societies without acknowledging the specificity of twentieth-century USA (Urry 2000b). Parsons defined 'society' as 'the type of social system characterized by the highest level of self-sufficiency relative to its environment, including other social systems' (1971: 8). But such self-sufficient societies are rare and almost always rely upon their domination of other societies, such as that effected by the USA during all of the twentieth century. And no analysis of social order could now be envisaged that does not address the immensely complex forms of global interdependence, economically, socially, politically, culturally and environmentally. Social order in one society always depends upon its multiple connections with emergent transnational relations.

Finally, it is now increasingly clear just how *social* order is not the outcome of purified *social* processes. As Law argues: 'the notion that social ordering is, indeed, simply social also disappears. . . . what we call the social is materially heterogeneous: talk, bodies, texts, machines, architectures, all of these and many more are implicated in and perform the social'(1994: 2). In that sense classical sociology's notion of accounting for a purified *social* order is past and should be relegated to the dustbin of history (Latour 1993; Knorr-Cetina 1997).

In this book I have elaborated some theoretical resources that break with such classical notions of social order. A number of claims have been advanced and defended. Thus criss-crossing 'societies' are diverse systems in complex interconnections with their environments. There are many chaotic effects that are distant in time–space from where they originate. These in part result from the positive as well as the negative feedback mechanisms that mean that order *and* chaos are always intertwined. There are many increasingly powerful self-organizing global networks and fluids that are moving systems far from equilibrium. And there is not a social order that can be accounted for by purified social processes.

Such complexity thinking enables our thinking to overcome the dichotomies of determinism and free will. We can begin to see how powerful material worlds are unpredictable, unstable, sensitive to initial conditions, irreversible and rarely 'societally' organized. Indeed, does this therefore mean, following former UK Prime Minister Margaret Thatcher, that 'there is no such thing as society'? Is there no longer a societal ordering, although Thatcher argued this for very different 'methodologically individualist' reasons?

This book seeks to show that there are 'societies', but that their societal capacity has been transformed through becoming elements within systems of global complexity. These systems possess no tendencies towards equilibrium and all sorts of social relationships get ineluctably drawn into the attractor of glocalization. There are various networks and fluids roaming the globe that, unlike societies, possess the power of rapid movement across, over and under many societies as 'regions' (see chapter 4 above; see also Bauman 2000).

I will now make a few comments about how societies are transformed by becoming elements within the systems of global complexity. For the past couple of centuries apparently separate 'societies' (especially those within the north Atlantic rim) have been characterized by a 'banal nationalism' that separated one from the other. A banal nationalism involves waving celebratory flags, singing national anthems, flying flags on nationally important public buildings, identifying with national sports heroes, being addressed in the media as a member of a given society, celebrating that society's independence day, sharing certain similar political and cultural practices and so on (Billig 1995). Many of these core components of such a nationalism date from the late nineteenth century.

The development of global complexity means that each such banal nationalism increasingly circulates along the global informational and communicational channels and systems. They become familiar to, and indeed part of, each society's branding, within the wider global order. Mega events increasingly occur when the nation and its 'banal' characteristics are placed upon the world's stage for display and consumption, especially through the global fluid of 'travelling peoples'. Each such banal nationalism is increasingly consumed by others, compared and evaluated, and turned into a brand. We might say that there is a move from banal nationalism to brand nationalism in the new global order, especially at moments of global celebration and consumption (Roche 2000).

Indeed, I noted above that there are thought to be at least 2,000 'nation peoples' all suffering various kinds of displacement and ambiguous location (R. Cohen 1997: pp. ix–x; Papastergiadis 2000). Only a minority of 'societies' are constituted as apparently separate nation state societies. Most societies are not nations, let alone nation states, the most striking of such non-nation-state societies being the 'overseas Chinese'. Each is increasingly drawn into the attractor and gets rebranded within global complexity. More-over, in many places people develop multiple identities, since often there is no longer the one 'true national self'. Over half of those living in Scotland consider themselves Scottish *and* British (McCrone 1998: 140).

Mike Davis's *Magical Urbanism* (2000b) brings out some extra-ordinary dimensions of the fluid diaspora of the thirty-two million or so Latinos now living within the USA. They are the largest ethnic group in Los Angeles, forming a city within a city, and they will soon outnumber whites living in California. Or, to put it dif-ferently, US Latinos are already the fifth largest 'nation' within Latin America. There are wide-ranging processes of 'cultural syn-cretism that may become a transformative template for the whole society' as the USA is becoming inexorably Latinized (Davis 2000b: 15). Much of this syncretism stems from 'transnational-ized communities' moving between especially Mexico, now very much a 'nomadic' country, and the USA: 'like quantum particles in two places at once' (Davis 2000b: 77). Levitt (2001) somewhat similarly describes the self-organizing 'transnational villages' formed by those living more or less simultaneously in the USA and the Dominican Republic. There is an extensive transnational-ism from below.

This system of global complexity is thus comprised of many different 'islands of order', a notion elaborated in chapter 5. There are not only national societies and complex hybrid diasporas, but other networked/fluid polities including 'supra-national states', global religions or 'civilizations', international organizations, inter-national meetings, NGOs and cross-border regions (Perkmann 2000; Duffield 2001; Habermas 2001; ch. 4; Walby forthcoming).

Any society as a particular bounded territory typically finds diverse self-organizing 'polities' seeking to striate its space, subjecting it to diverse forms of social regulation. In particular, according to Deleuze and Guattari, nation states are necessarily involved in seeking to regulate those numerous mobilities that move in and across such spaces. One of the fundamental tasks of the state is, they say,

> to striate the space over which it reigns. . . . It is a vital concern of
> every State not only to vanquish nomadism, but to control migra-

tions and, more generally, to establish a zone of rights over an entire 'exterior', over all the flows traversing the ecumenon. If it can help it, the State does not dissociate itself from a process of capture of flows of all kinds, populations, commodities, money or capital, etc. . . . the State never ceases to decompose, recompose and transform movement, or to regulate speed. (Deleuze and Guattari 1986: 59–60)

But global complexity means that states have increasingly shifted away from governing a relatively fixed and clear-cut national population resident within its territory and constituting a distinct and relatively unchanging community of fate (Urry 2000b: ch. 8). Shifts towards global networks and fluids transform the space beyond each state that they have to striate. Habermas argues that '"globalization" conjures up images of overflowing rivers, washing away all the frontier checkpoints and controls, and ultimately the bulwark of the nation itself' (2001: 67). States thus can be said increasingly to act as a legal, economic and social regulator, or gamekeeper, of practices and mobilities that are predominantly provided by, or generated through, the often unpredictable consequences of many other entities. Social regulation is both necessitated by, and is only made possible through, new computer-based forms of information gathering, retrieval and dissemination. Such databases can refer to almost every economic and social institution. Such internationalized information flows derive from the emergence of a widespread 'audit society', a subset of the vision machines that ubiquitous computing ushers in (Power 1994).

Thus one paradoxical consequence of the intensely fluid and turbulent nature of the global complexity is that 'the role of the state is actually becoming more, rather than less, important in developing the productive powers of territory and in producing new spatial configurations' (Swyngedouw 1992: 431). One further consequence is that states are not converging in a uniform powerless direction but are becoming much more diverse, from the Taliban to the EU to the USA (Weiss 1998: ch. 7). Indeed, there has been an 'enormous expansion of nation-state structures, bureaucracies, agenda, revenues and regulatory capacities since World War II', in order to deal with global fluids such as information flows, travelling peoples, international terrorism, health and environmental risks and so on that all move across borders in dizzying and transmutating form (Meyer et al. 1997: 157). Keil (1998) summarizes such developments by maintaining that globalization produces new kinds of 'states'.

In some ways nation states across Europe are becoming more like the European Union. The EU is organized around the promotion of various mobilities. It has sought to develop the four freedoms of movement – of goods, services, labour and capital – and has intervened with national state policies to eliminate many barriers to mobility, trade and competition. The EU can be seen as a 'regulatory state', mostly involved in the monitoring and regulation of the policies and practices of its individual nation states that have freely joined up (Majone 1994, 1996). Its Treaties and Directives are particularly powerful. They mean both that governments must bring their own legislation in line with such Treaties, and that individual citizens in the EU can appeal direct to the European Court of Justice when it is believed that national governments have not implemented appropriate policies (Walby 1999). Significantly, European laws take precedence over national laws where they conflict and it is possible for the actions of individual governments to be declared illegal.

Some states, such as the EU, indeed function as what we might call 'midwives' for developing and enhancing global networks and fluids and are not merely subjected to them. And states increasingly act as catalysts of networks of countries operating at the regional or international level and hence function as one class of agencies in a more dynamic system of unpredictable global complexity (Hirst and Thompson 1996: ch. 8). Castells (1996, 1997) more generally talks of the increasingly networked character of states. There are many international conferences and events that involve individual states forming, negotiating and signing up to international agreements that then have the further effect of promoting and performing the global (such as the 1997 Kyoto Protocol on climate change). There has also been the growth of 'networked wars' and indeed of what we might call 'networked terrorists' (Duffield 2001).

There is also heightened mediatization such that regulatory failure of individual states can be brought into the open, made visible, and individuals and organizations can be shamed by the ensuing scandals or threat of scandals. States indeed can be subject to 'mediated scandals', scandals that interestingly reveal substantial restructurings in the very complexities of power.

Power and Complexity

Much thinking about power in the social sciences has been focused upon the interrelationships between apparently powerful and apparently powerless agents. Power is conceptualized as attributes of agents, through observing two or more human agents and seeing in what ways, and to what degree, the actions of each are influenced by that of the other. If one agent is able to get the other to do something that he or she would not otherwise do, then that is deemed to be an exercise of power. Steven Lukes's *Power: A Radical View* (1973) famously critiques this intersubjective conception of power through advocating a three-dimensional view based upon 'real interests'. Lukes shows how the most effective exercise of power occurs when there is no overt or even covert bending of the will of one agent by that of the other. Power is exercised if people's real interests are secured and this is best realized without overt or covert intersubjective competition and struggle. Power is thus conceived of as structural and not intersubjective. However, this argument has remained partly buried, because Lukes uses the language of Marxism to identify 'real' as opposed to expressed or visible interests or 'false consciousness'. But what is notable in Lukes's account is his critique of the subject-oriented position and his advocacy of the analysis of 'domination' as opposed to that of 'power' (A. Stewart 2001).

But in much social science power conceived as a property of agents remains central to the analysis of social relations. In the end power is often seen to involve human agents appearing able to get their way, forcing the other who is in some ways co-present to do something that he or she would not otherwise do, to be able to bend the will of this other. Power gets attached to agency in the couplet agency-structure.

However, many developments described in this book subvert this very distinction between agency and structure. Complexity transcends the division between free will and determinism and

hence between agency and structure. It transcends the characteristic way in which power has been located, as agency. So what
then would constitute a complexity approach to power?

Power would not be regarded as a thing or a possession. It is
something that flows or runs and may be increasingly detached
from specific territory or space. It is non-contiguous. Bauman
(2000: 10–14) outlines and defends a 'post-panoptical' conception of power. Power is not necessarily exercised through actual
co-presence as one agent gets another to do what he or she would
otherwise not have done through interpersonal threat, force or
persuasion. But also power no longer necessarily involves imagined co-presence within a literal or simulated panopticon where
the powerless are actually or potentially visible to the powerful.

By contrast, Bauman suggests that the prime technique of
power now is that of 'escape, slippage, elision and avoidance', the
'end of the era of mutual engagement' (2000: 11). Modern societies had involved a mixture of citizenship with settlement and
hence with co-presence within the confines of a specific territori-
ally based society. But now the new global elite, according to
Bauman, can rule 'without burdening itself with the chores of
administration, management, welfare concerns', even involving
developing disposable slave owning without commitment (2000:
13; on 'disposable peoples', see Bales 1999). Travelling light is the
new asset of power. Power is all about speed, lightness, distance,
the weightless, the global, and this is true both of elites and of
those resisting elites such as anti-globalization protestors or terrorists. Power runs in and especially jumps across the different
global networks and fluids. Power is hybridized and is not simply
social but material.

In particular, citizenship and social order have always depended
upon relations of mutual *visibility* between the citizen and the state.
In medieval and early modern societies, the theatrical, co-present
visibility of the monarch to his or her court was central to the maintenance of society's symbolic order and power relations. The ritual
procession or 'progress' of the king or queen around his or her
kingdom further served to constitute his or her wider subjects as a
community of direct *watchers* of power. With the emergence of
modern societies especially from the eighteenth century onwards,
the economy of visibility between citizen and state transmutes

(Thompson 1995: ch. 4; Szerszynski and Urry 2001). Citizens are now not just watchers but objects of state surveillance and monitoring; there is a generalized increase in 'visual reflexivity'; public authorities are increasingly expected to provide open and transparent forms of behaviour; there are new forms of 'impression management' in reaction to increased media visibility; and 'mediated scandals' grow more significant (Foucault 1977; Meyrowitz 1985).

By the twenty-first century citizens are subject to informational mediated power, forms of power that are complex in their mechanisms and consequences. On the one hand, there are extraordinary new forms of *informational and mediated* power with the development of vision machines, the tens of thousands of satellites, bugs, listening devices, the microscopic cameras, CCTV, the Internet, the possibilities of sharing information, GIS/GPS and so on. And, on the other hand, the mobilities of everyday life involve speed, lightness and distance, and the capacity to move unnoticed through even the most surveyed of societies, such as by transmutating from student to tourist to terrorist back to student and so on.

Informational and mediated power is mobile, performed and unbounded. This is its strength and its vulnerability. Attempted ordering even by the most powerful can result in an array of complex unintended effects that take the system away from equilibrium. In such unpredictable and irreversible transformations, power, and especially mediated power, is like sand. It may stay resolutely in place, forming itself into clear and bounded shapes, with a distinct spatial topology waiting say to be arrested or bombed, or it may turn into an avalanche and race away, sweeping much else in its wake.

This unpredictability of power, its capacity to transmute from form to form, its capacity to be nowhere or everywhere, will now be illustrated through examining some aspects of the contemporary phenomenon of scandal.

The Complexity of Scandal

The late-twentieth-century emergence of a 'mediated power' criss-crossing the globe produced distinctly new forms of mediated scandals. The complex scandal of power and the power of scandal can be viewed through John Thompson's *Political Scandal: Power and Visibility in the Media Age* (2000).

The global media disembed events from local contexts and move them, often instantaneously and simultaneously, across the globe. At the same time, the breaking-down of more solid class-based forms of politics means that relationships in most countries and regions are less organized and more fluid and mobile – more wave-like – and hence these scandal events can more rapidly emerge, and pass in, through and beyond the frontiers of given societies.

Four processes in combination generate 'complexity' outcomes with regard to contemporary scandals. These are normative transgressions, the significance and vulnerability of trust, the fact of exposure and the power to make events instantaneously and simultaneously visible.

First, then, globally mediated scandals occur where there are significant transgressions of particular *norms* of 'expected behaviour' that characterize a given society or type of society. According to Thompson, these transgressions normally relate to sexual behaviour, to financial matters or to the use/abuse of power. Given the ambivalent, contested and often quite strict norms relating to public figures and institutions, then 'scandalous' transgressions regularly occur (as most citizens are well aware!). There are many potential scandals, especially since public figures and institutions are normally confronted by stricter norms of what is appropriate behaviour than those not in the mediatized 'public' eye. But the public eye seduces increasing numbers of new 'subjects' into the visual media and who are then subject to cycles of transgression, revelation and confession (what we might term Big Brother narcissism).

Second, the power of certain incumbents of official positions, of companies and of states, rests upon a 'politics of *trust*'. With particular incumbents such trust is based on their presumed character rather than on specific skills. Sometimes there appears to be a kind of 'global trust' (such as that enjoyed on occasions by the President of the USA, the General-Secretary of the UN, Nelson Mandela, certain states, certain global companies and so on). But such trust has to be continuously earned or performed and hence it can rapidly erode. There is much to lose, especially where trust and character are core to the establishment and maintenance of the legitimacy of an incumbent or organization. And, the greater the trust, the more that character has been put on line, then the greater is any ensuing scandal (other things being equal). Trust is an exceptionally strong but an incredibly brittle resource. It has to be continuously performed. If it stops being earned, then it will erode instantaneously, as with an individual whose character or good name gets exposed and subject to scandal. Trust may disappear overnight. As those subject to scandal often say, they took years building up their good 'name' but 'their world collapsed overnight' as the scandal 'swept' over both them and their unfortunate friends and family.

Third, there is the power of *exposure*. This involves the making of the private transgressive act transparent to the public and hence just that: public (Meyerowitz 1985; Balkin 1999). The wide-ranging global media increasingly possess the techniques to make transparent what the powerful would mostly seek to maintain as 'private'. Such media employ technologies of observation, surveillance and monitoring of people within their supposedly 'private' lives. These technologies were initially developed within the secret services of states, such as eavesdropping, phone tapping, secret cameras, listening devices, telephoto lenses, computer hacking, stalking and so on (with Watergate, of course, it was Nixon's own tapes that provided his downfall). But the power of exposure is to make what is supposedly backstage or 'private', frontstage or 'public'. And with digitization there are few if any images of the private that can ever be 'locked away' for good, that will remain forever private and opaque. Hoskins (2001: 218) analyses the power of the 'hidden' media images of the Lewinksy–Clinton embraces that were then endlessly replayed once the scandal had broken.

Fourth, there is the attractor of *visibility or transparency*. Mediatization involves the enhanced visualization of power. People and organizations across the globe are drawn into the ambit of visibility and its seductive charms so as to be famous for fifteen minutes. And it is bodies that are made especially visible through mediatized visibility, bodies that speak to the world both intimately and 'close up' and yet simultaneously to vast numbers. This produces a distinct kind of performative biopower, an embodied power or a 'public intimacy' through figures made visible and revealed on the world's media. But this immense biopower is exceptionally vulnerable – to exposure, as 'figures' of power can suddenly, overnight, be seen (through) as flawed, as bodily scandalous. All those watching on the media can bear witness to the public shaming, the making transparent, of the transgresser and on occasions their public confession. Gitlin (1980) described this as *The Whole World is Watching*. The exposed individuals, companies or states are revealed, their scandalness is made visible and their biopower dissolves in front of the world's gaze.

Moreover, the competitive nature of the overlapping and digitized media enhances the attractor of transparency. Competition enables the figure of the 'wrongdoer' to be revealed, replayed again and again, and his or her global shame made visible before, and endlessly repeated across, the globe. This was paradigmatically seen with former President Clinton and the fascination with his immense but vulnerable biopower.

Scandals, we might say, involve small causes (the furtive embrace, the tiny lie, the small payment, the handwritten note). These small causes can, in very particular circumstances, produce distant and catastrophic consequences for those involved and for many others drawn into the swirling vortex of a scandalizing event. Events are typically unpredictable, with no one able to control the trajectory of a scandal (Thompson 2000: 75). There are unexpected, unpredictable and uncontrollable visibilities as images flow within, and rapidly jump across, the various media. The media compete for global stories and produce what Balkin (1999: 402) terms a 'cascade effect'. Different journalists with diverse standards of journalistic integrity compete with each other for further scandals to reveal. Especially crucial in producing such cascades are visual images that disrupt or ridicule or overturn existing relations of biopower. Such images get endlessly sold and resold across the globe, as they subvert, humiliate and transgress the apparent power of the powerful. Those who live by the media can also die a horrible death through such mediated cascades.

Scandals thus involve complex sets of events that are unpredictable *and* irreversible. They run out of control once there is exposure, because of the mobility and speed of the processes of exposure, visualization and recirculation. The irreversible events lead away from equilibrium, especially where those involved try to manage events, to cover their tracks, to lay the ghost to rest. There are powerful positive feedback mechanisms where character and trust dissolve almost overnight and the shame is massively enhanced and magnified. In complexity mode, most attempts to minimize exposure will result in the enlargement of the scandal, especially with the further scandal of 'concealment'. Efforts to dampen down the evolving events produce complex magnification with diverse and further irreversible consequences.

Indeed, once the media have peered 'backstage' then there is escalating exposure and visualization of the scandalous figures. Balkin (1999: 402) describes the 'self-amplifying focus' of a media feeding 'frenzy' that takes root and leaves little standing in its whirlwind path. Scandals can possess a kind of all-consuming flow that can 'wash' over those caught up in its wake. As Thompson (2000: 85) argues, 'the experience is likely to be overwhelming, as events rapidly spin out of control', away from any movement towards equilibrium.

'Financial' and 'abuse of power' scandals are particularly interesting in that they often occur at moments of global scrutiny conducted in, and through, the world's media. Especially significant are those big public meetings when the company or country brand is put on display and revealed to the world (Stevenson 1997: 46; Klein 2000). In a single week in the 1990s, Rio Tinto, Shell, Premier Oil, Nestlé and ICI all held Annual General Meetings in which groups of protesters mobilized the world's media to expose and to shame these companies for their misdeeds.

Significantly, these normative transgressions often and unpredictably occurred in countries far away from where the AGM was actually held. But, of course, with instant communications there is often 'no hiding place'. The brand in question gets threatened with exposure and shame at the very moment that it is being presented upon the world's stage. The power of a brand can evaporate rapidly. The example of Nike, and the threatening of its brand because of the 'slave wages' paid to its workforce, show that 'public shaming and consumer pressure can have a mighty impact upon mighty manufacturers' (Dionne 1998: 11; see also Klein 2000).

Thus liquid mediated power is a key component transforming power relations in the global age. Such symbolic power flows across national borders through the world's media and informational channels. And, as it flows, it is both performed and can be undermined (Thompson 2000: 246–8). An incumbent's good name (Clinton), the 'brand' of a state (USA and its refusal to sign up to Kyoto/Bonn) or the 'brand' of a corporation (Nike) all constitute extremely powerful *and* yet extremely vulnerable symbolic capital. As power is increasingly exercised through the performativity of character, brand and name, these can be threatened and destroyed through exposure and shame. As scandals get instantaneously transmitted across the globe, they threaten such power. Those incumbents, companies or states that live by such power can also, through complex, irreversible, fluid and far-from-equilibrium processes, die a lingering, transparent and utterly captivating death from it. Attempts at producing order spin out of control and destroy most of those caught up in the swirling vortex of scandal that can drag down the powerful, their circle and much else besides.

Indeed, the occurrence of specific scandals is generating a more general 'culture of scandal' within highly mediated capitalist societies, especially the USA. Balkin (1999: 406) describes this irreversibly developing culture as being like a 'mutating virus', constantly changing its features in order to grow more widely and to spread more quickly. Scandals produce new kinds of TV programme, new modes of journalistic reporting, new web sites, new modes of media competition. These have the unintended emergent effect through positive feedback that: 'Like a particularly obnoxious weed in a field of grass, the culture of scandal gradually pushes aside other discourses and threatens to consume a greater and greater share of public attention, public discussion and public opinion' (Balkin 1999: 207). So what began as the democratic attempt to reveal the many transgressions of the powerful unpredictably turns out to produce a culture that can drive out almost all forms of media reporting that do not display and enhance the virulent culture of scandal.

Conclusion

This chapter has examined a variety of mobile processes that make social order contingent and unusual. Societies have been shown to be increasingly components within various systems of global complexity. The discussion of scandal shows that forms of informational and mediated power are mobile, performed and unbounded. This provides both their strength but also their vulnerability. Attempted ordering even by the most powerful within societies can result in complex unintended effects that take the system in question further away from equilibrium.

In such unpredictable and irreversible transformations, power, and especially mediated power, is, we have seen, like sand. It may stay resolutely in place forming clear and bounded shapes or it may turn into an avalanche and race away sweeping much else in its wake. What Bauman terms 'liquid modernity' is full of unexpected, unpredictable and irreversible movements, including the more recent emergence of a culture of scandal that takes social life further away from points of equilibrium.

In the next chapter I return to some implications of global complexity for sociology and its characteristic theories of the social world. And I go on to explore some implications of machines, empires and the cosmopolitan for the strangely ordered world that seems simultaneously to be on the edge of chaos.

7

Global Complexities

Complexity and Social Theory

Auguste Comte famously described sociology as 'social physics'. Whether or not that was a helpful suggestion in the nineteenth century, I have argued that at the beginning of the twenty-first century we should consider the relevance of the physics of complexity for contemporary sociology/social science. This has not been much debated. Most claims for the social science relevance of complexity involve rather particularistic accounts within specific social spheres (see on urban patterns, Byrne 1998; on strikes, Biggs 1998; on social policy, Medd 2000).

Moreover, the main critique of its potential relevance, P. Stewart's recent argument that social phenomena 'are too complex for complexity theory to deal with' (2001: 353), does not consider the potential of complexity. Stewart considers whether it already constitutes a complete social theory. That is surely the wrong question, since no one would imagine that it is already formed as such a theory. In *The Hidden Connections*, complexity-theorist Fritjof Capra (2002) develops an analysis of the social that we might say 'takes off' from complexity but does not reduce social life to dynamic systems.

Furthermore, physical science models should not be directly transplanted into the social sciences since we are now better aware of the complicated relations between models and the phenomena that they purport to characterize. Unforeseen 'chaotic' consequences can result from drawing strict analogies between models of phenomena developed within different domains of enquiry. However, given the necessarily metaphorical nature of all science, this book has considered whether complexity could generate productive metaphors for the social analysis of various 'post-societal' material worlds. I follow complexity-theorist Brian Arthur's views that complexity writers are 'beginning to develop metaphors' and that the Santa Fe Institute 'is in the business of formulating the metaphors for this new science, metaphors that, with luck, will guide the way these sciences are done over the next fifty years of so' (1994b: 680). Complexity thus seeks to establish pattern similarity operating within and across many different systems, whether they are nominally 'physical' or 'human'.

Special focus has been placed here upon the metaphors appropriate for examining the material worlds implicated in the apparent 'globalization' of economic, social, political, cultural and environmental relationships. In the past decade the social science of the global has extensively described many of these relationships. However, much social science has not developed complex analysis of global systems that transcend the societal or national. It has tended to take the global for granted and then shown how, and in what ways, various localities, regions, nation states, environments and cultures have been transformed in linear fashion by this all-powerful entity that many call 'globalization'. Thus globalization (or sometimes global capitalism) has come to be viewed as the new 'structure', with localities, regions and so on as the new 'agent'.

However, I have shown the limitations of the structure/agency divide, drawing in part upon Giddens's 'duality of structure' thesis (1984). This structurationist formulation breaks with linear notions, since it sees the rules and resources of systems both being drawn upon by knowledgeable agents and then feeding back through actions to reproduce system rules and resources. In Giddens's account there are not fixed and separate entities possessing variable characteristics. There is some appreciation of relationality. Moreover, functionalist arguments partly presuppose a non-linear account, since there are circular negative feedback mechanisms in which 'causes' and 'effects' are in effect co-present within the functionally integrated 'system'.

But this book uses complexity to move beyond various positions within social theory. I have sought to show that there is no 'structure' and no 'agency', no 'macro' and no 'micro' levels, no 'societies' and no 'individuals', and no 'system world' and no 'life world'. This is because each such notion presumes that there are entities with separate and distinct essences that are then brought into external juxtaposition with its other. Structurationist and functionalist approaches have also been critiqued for relatively simple formulations of a finalized and reproduced social order, towards which social processes necessarily move.

Overall my argument here is one that rests upon a profound 'relationality'. This position is also central to actor-network theory (Law and Mol 2000), to various post-structuralist formulations (Dillon 2000) and to critics of generalized linear reality (Abbott 2001). Dillon (2000: 12) maintains that: 'No party to a relation is therefore a monadic, or molar, entity. Each is, instead, a mutable function of the character of the mode-of-being-related and its capacity for relationality' (see also Emirbayer 1997). Relationality is brought about through a wide array of networked or circulating relationships that are implicated within different overlapping and increasingly convergent *material* worlds. In examining such material worlds I have noted what Clark (2000: 31) describes as the 'porosity between the study of the social and the study of the natural that corresponds to the openness of the human organism to the greater flux of energy, matter and life'.

The linear metaphor of scales, such as that stretching from the micro level to the macro level, or from the life world to the system world, which has plagued social theory from its inception, should thus be replaced by the metaphor of connections. Such connections are to be viewed as more or less intense, more or less mobile, more or less social and more or less 'at a distance' (see Dicken et al. 2001: 102–4; on system/life worlds, see Sayer 2000). Latour maintains that the social 'possesses the bizarre property of not being made of agency or structure at all, but rather of being a *circulating* entity' (1999: 17). There are many trajectories or movements that are neither macro nor micro but circulate between each in terms of 'speed; velocity; waves; continuous flow; pulsing; fluidity and viscosity; rhythm; harmony; discordance; and turbulence' (Dillon 2000: 12). There is therefore no top or bottom of society, but many connections or circulations that effect relationality through performances at multiple and varied distances. Latour maintains that 'there is no zoom going from macro structure to micro interactions . . . [since] both micro and macro are local effects of hooking up to circulating entities' (1999: 19).

This book is, therefore, concerned with the systemic non-linear relationships of global complexity that transcend most conventional divides of social science. It is concerned with examining 'mobile connections'. Some formulations from complexity have been drawn upon to advance the analysis of non-equilibrium conditions of global ordering. There are various characteristics of this 'complex' relationality.

First, the very large number of elements makes such systems unpredictable and lacking any finalized 'order'. These elements interact physically and, because of various dematerializing transformations, informationally over multiple time–spaces. They are irreversibly drawn towards various 'attractors' that exercise a kind of gravity effect, especially what I have termed the glocalization attractor. Interactions are complex, rich and non-linear, involving multiple negative and, more significantly, positive feedback loops with ineluctable patterns of increasing returns and path dependence. Such systems interact dissipatively with their environment. The elements within any such system operate under conditions that are far from equilibrium, partly because each element responds only to 'local' sources of information. But elements at one location have very significant time–space effects elsewhere through multiple connections and trajectories. There can be a profound disproportionality of 'causes' and 'effects'. Such systems possess a history that irreversibly evolves and where past events are thus never 'forgotten'. Points of bifurcation may be reached when the system branches. And the various sciences are themselves powerful elements within such systems and have unpredictable and irreversible effects upon systemic development, especially on the character and development of global systems. Such systems should never be seen as involving *simply* linear increases in the colonization of the life world, or of enhanced agency, or of greater risk.

This then comprises a significant array of general claims. I have tried to make some contribution to the further development of the social sciences of complexity with analyses of the material worlds implicated within processes of global ordering. Further topics where I think subsequent writers could also work would be, first, the enhancement of some complexity methods, data sets and simulation techniques that are apposite to 'social life'. Further, it would be desirable to develop formal methods for specifying the boundaries, limits and consequences of different kinds of networks, especially what I have termed GINs and GFs. And, most ambitiously, complexity notions should be seen as the basis of a thoroughgoing post-disciplinarity appropriate to the diverse material worlds currently moving across the globe (see http://www.math. uptras.gr/~mboudour/). Such post-disciplinarity would involve systematic analyses to transcend the physical science/social science divide.

Machines

This book has particularly emphasized the apparently more 'liquid' character of contemporary global relations, involving the dematerializing of information and the unpredictable and speeded up character of networked and fluid relationships, whether of money, risks, tourism, terrorism or information. Indeed, key to examining the global are the wide array of global networks and global fluids that occupy complex, contradictory and irreversible relationships with each other. Some features of these have been elaborated; they constitute what I called, following Prigogine, 'pools of order' within increasing disorder. Their importance means that linear accounts of the global, such as those that point to increasing wealth, or homogenization, or democracy, or violence, are wrong. All such processes are to be found, but they are hugely interdependent with each other, each providing the conditions under which their 'other' develops.

But why is this? Why does not the increasingly 'liquid' character of the global world mean that relationality is simply unproblematic? Why does not 'liquid modernity', as Bauman (2000) characterizes the contemporary world, generate mobile solutions to system 'failings'? The answer is that those mobilities connecting the local and global always depend upon multiple stabilities.

Deterritorialization presupposes reterritorialization, as Lefebvre (1991) consistently shows (see also Brenner 1999b: 435–6; 1999a). The complex character of such systems stems from the multiple time–space fixities or moorings that enable the fluidities of liquid modernity to be realized. Thus 'mobile machines', such as mobile phones, cars, aircraft, trains, and computer connections, all presume overlapping and varied time–space immobilities (see Graham and Marvin 2001).

This relationality between mobilites and immobilities is a typical complexity characteristic. There is no linear increase in fluidity without extensive systems of immobilities. Thus the so-far most powerful mobile machine, the aeroplane, requires the largest and most extensive immobility, of the airport city employing tens of thousands of workers (on the complex nature of such multiple 'airspaces', see Pascoe 2001). The least powerful mobile machine, human legs, requires almost no such immobilities (except maybe the armchair!). I now outline various immobilities involved here.

1   There are *temporary* moments of rest of a machine and/or its users and/or its messages, such as at a bus stop, voice mailbox, passport control, railway station or web site. The machine or its object or user waits in preparation for its next mobile phase.
2   There are short periods of *storage*, such as the overnight stay of a car in a garage or an aircraft on an airfield or information within a database or a passenger within a motel. Such modes of temporary storage often involve complex sorting and stacking procedures.
3   There is the *long-term infrastructural* immobility – of airports or CCTV cameras or railway lines or pylons or satellites that orchestrate the intermittent mobilities through a literal path dependency.
4   There is the *inter-generational disposal* of the materials from 'dead' machines, such as the transforming of immobile train carriages or cars or landlines into 'disposed' waste and recycled materials.
5   These mobilities are hugely *uneven* in time–space, so that some zones are rich with movement and some are movement poor, and in fact become relatively poor as mobilities happen

elsewhere (see Graham and Marvin 2001). States are centrally implicated in seeking to increase movements within and across certain zones and in compensating for the massive consequences of overlapping zones of relative immobility.

There are therefore specialized *periods* and *places* involving temporary rest, storage, infra-structural immobility, disposal and immobile zones. How, when and where these materialize are of immense systemic consequence, relating to the organization of time–space. The intersections of these periods and places facilitate or preclude the apparently seamless mobilities of people, information, objects and equipment across time–space. Overall it is these moorings that enable movement. And it is the dialectic of mobility/moorings that produces social complexity. If all relationality were mobile or 'liquid', then there would be no complexity. Complexity, I suggest, stems from this dialectic of mobility and moorings.

There have, moreover, been significant transformations in the operation of this dialectic over time. This can be seen by briefly considering the changing nature of 'machines'. The nineteenth century was the century of 'industrial machines', machines that mainly made other machines or material objects or that transported such machines or objects. Each technology developed relatively independently, although a key development was the emergence of *steam* power. Experts, who were often experts in that machine itself and not in other machines, inhabited these industrial machines.

The twentieth century was the era of 'familial machines' and of 'war machines'. Family household members inhabited familial machines, including white-space goods, the family car, telephone, the radio, the household TV/VCR, the PC, heating appliances and the camera/camcorder. Such machines were mainly stored within the home/garage and helped to form twentieth-century family life. Most family members could operate most of these domesticated machines. These machines depended wholly or partly upon *electric* power, except strangely for the car. Twentieth-century 'war machines' were non-domesticated, and included, besides technologies of mass destruction, various spin-offs such as jet transport, nuclear energy, space travel for science, and virtual reality for simulations of work and science. These machines were stored in highly specialized camps or bases where the public was forbidden and which had enhanced systems of surveillance.

The twenty-first century will be the century of what I call 'inhabited machines'. These are machines that are dwelt in by single individuals or by very small groups. Such inhabited machines are miniaturized, privatized, mobilized and depend upon *digital* power. This power is substantially separate from material form and involves exceptional levels of miniaturization and mobility. Many of these machines are portable, carried around by 'digital nomads' (Makimoto and Manners 1997). Such machines are desired for their style, smallness and lightness and demonstrate a physical form closely interwoven with the corporeal. Early examples include walkmans, new generation mobile phones, the individual TV, the networked computer/Internet, the individualized smart car, virtual reality 'travel', smart small personal aircraft and others yet to emerge. These machines involve interesting reconfigurations of storage: the portals to these machines are carried around with the individual, they are stored on or close to the person and yet their digital power derives from their extensive connectivity.

These inhabiting machines enable 'people' to be more readily mobile through space, or to stay in one place because of the capacity for 'self-retrieval' of personal information at other times or spaces. Through such machines people inhabit global networks and fluids of information, image and movement. 'Persons' thus occur as various nodes in these multiple machines of inhabitation and mobility. The storage in such machines is digitized and hence is not only 'just in time' but also 'just in space'. There is a person-to-person connectivity that represents a further shift in the dematerialization of information and mobility discussed in chapter 4 (see Wellman 2001). The global fluids of 'travelling peoples', 'Internet' and 'information' increasingly overlap and converge, generating irreversible changes that further move social life towards what Wellman (2001) terms 'personalized networking'. This involves the further linking-together of 'physical space' and 'cyberspace'. This convergence across the various global fluids further transcends divisions of structure and agency, the global and the local.

Clearly these globally complex mobility developments have major implications for the concept of society that has been discursively central to the sociological project (Urry 2000b: ch. 1). I finish this book by turning to two recent debates, around 'empire' and around the 'cosmopolitan', which are both concerned to theorize the emergent nature of the 'post-society' era that we appear to be moving towards. I examine some significant global complexities of that era.

Empires and Multitudes

In *Empire*, Michael Hardt and Antonio Negri (2000) argue that the concept of 'empire' or 'imperial sovereignty' has replaced that of nation-state sovereignty. By 'empire' they mean the emergence of a dynamic and flexible systemic structure articulated horizontally across the globe, a kind of 'governance without government' that sweeps together all actors within the order as a whole (Hardt and Negri 2000: 13–14). Empire is the sovereign power, a 'smooth world', the single logic of rule that now governs the world. This new global form of sovereignty is deterritorialized and decentred, with a merging and blending of a 'global rainbow' (Hardt and Negri 2000: p. xiii). There is no centre of power and no fixed boundaries or barriers. The 'age of globalization is the age of universal contagion' (Hardt and Negri 2000: 136). And 'empire' crucially generates its opposite, what Hardt and Negri describe as 'the resistances, struggles and desires of the [mobile] multitude' that constitutes the 'other' to empire (2000: pp. xvi, 398).

Such a notion of 'empire' parallels my argument as to the centrality of the deterritorialized and decentred mobilities of the global system. However, there is little specification by Hardt and Negri of the *systemic* relations within 'empire' and especially how it operates in conditions far from equilibrium. Theirs is a remarkably undynamic account of self-reproducing global relations. They say, for example, that empire 'is emerging today as the center that supports the globalization of productive networks' (Hardt and Negri 2000: 20). Empire here is conceived of functionally.

However, the research on global relations suggests that what Hardt and Negri call 'empire' needs to be analysed as much more institutionally and associationally 'complex' (as in Held et al. 1999). Further, they do not explain what happens to nation states or to 'societies' within such an 'empire'. It is as though, once nation states are no longer powerful forms of sovereignty, then there are no longer societies. All they imply is empire.

Thus the concept of 'empire' deployed by Hardt and Negri does not sufficiently capture the dynamic properties of global relations that only in part can be characterized as 'a sovereign power that governs the world' (2000: p. xi). Although Hardt and Negri conceptualize 'empire' as decentred and deterritorialized, they do not examine the array of interdependent fluid global hybrids that both make up and problematize their claim that 'there is world order' (2000: 3).

Rather, I suggest that the concept of 'empire' is a useful one, but not to characterize overall global relations. My analysis of global complexity suggests that all societies could be said to be becoming more *like* 'empires'. Contemporary societies possess an increasingly visible centre, with icons of power such as buildings, landscapes and brands, while beyond the centre there is a spreading of effects outwards with a relative weakness of borders. Within such 'empires' there are emergent inequalities rather than, as in at least welfare societies, an attempt to create citizenship rights that are common throughout the territory. In particular, societies are on the world's stage, showing off their trophies, competing with each other for the best skyline, palaces, galleries, stadia, infrastructures and so on, and seeking to avoid scandal and risk.

Societies are endlessly drawn into the glocal attractor and it is this that remakes them as 'empires', the USA being the most powerful and dominant of such societal empires currently strutting the world's stage. The USA possesses a number of exceptional centres (NY, LA, Washington), many icons of power (Pentagon, Wall Street, Hollywood, Ivy League Universities, Texan oil wells, Silicon Valley, MOMA), a porosity of borders (on the USA's Latinization, see Davis 2000b) and huge 'imperial' economic and social inequalities. It is the paradigm case of 'society as empire'. Thus, rather than there being a single 'empire', global complexity suggests that each society is drawn into the attractor of glocalization and is remade, so developing some characteristics of 'empire'.

And each society qua empire produces *its* opposite, its other, its rebellious multitude. And the globalizing of capitalist markets has generated some striking new zones from which 'multitudes' emerge to challenge empires. The events of 11 September seem to have emerged unpredictably from one of the very poorest countries in the world, and yet are said to have irreversibly changed many parameters structuring economic, social and political life. 11 September demonstrates the complexity of 'asymmetric threats', that 'wars' are increasingly fought between formally unequal powers with the apparently weak able to inflict massive blows on the apparently powerful. It is almost the secular equivalent of 'the first shall be last, and the last shall be first'. The mightier is the power of society as empire, the greater the harm that can be inflicted.

Global complexity can thus be seen in the power of the powerless to inflict the utmost harm upon the institutions of imperial power, especially those buildings, institutions and people that symbolize the intense condensation of imperial power. The USA is the paradigm case of 'society as empire'. And it is the New York skyline that most graphically symbolizes its imperial power.

Moreover, huge transformations are taking place in the very production of 'empire and multitude' across the globe. This can be seen as a specific example of the glocalizing attractor. Bhabha summarizes how: 'The globe shrinks for those who own it; for the displaced or the dispossessed, the migrant or refugee, no distance is more awesome than the few feet across borders or frontiers' (1992: 88).

Indeed one effect of global markets is to generate 'wild zones' of the increasingly dispossessed. In parts of the former USSR, sub-Saharan Africa, the Balkans, central America and central Asia are zones that are places of absence, of gaps, of lack. Such zones possess weak states with very limited infrastructures, no monopoly of the means of coercion, barely functioning economies often dependent upon commodifying illegal materials, an imploded social structure and a relatively limited set of connections to the global order.

In the 'West' socio-spatial inequalities have remained largely invisible. There is a 'splintering urbanism', with the invisibility of the 'other' taken to extreme lengths in the 'gated' cities of North

America (Graham and Marvin 2001). There are gated communities, condominiums, shopping centres, theme parks, workplaces, campuses, airports, financial districts and so on. The gates separate out the safe zones from the wild and dangerous zones within the cities of the West. Such zones of the ungovernable, the poor and the dispossessed are found in many cities especially across the USA.

But, increasingly, the time-space edges of these safe and the wild are coming into strange and dangerous new juxtapositions even, or perhaps especially, in the West. The flows from the wild zones of people, risks, substances, images and so on increasingly slip under, over and through the safe gates, suddenly and chaotically eliminating the invisibilities that had kept the zones apart. Through money laundering, the drug trade, urban crime, asylum seeking, people smuggling, slave trading and urban terrorism, the spaces of the wild and the safe are chaotically juxtaposed.

In systems of global complexity, wild and safe zones have become highly proximate through the curvatures of time–space. There is 'time–space compression', not only of the capitalist world but also of the 'terrorist world'. Wild zones are now only a telephone call, an Internet connection or a plane ride away. Capitalist markets have brought the 'whole world' closer and this is especially and paradoxically true of those bent on its violent destruction and especially on destroying the dominance of 'Americans' within the global order. 11 September demonstrates this new curvature of space and time, as the few feet were dramatically transcended and invisibility was no more. Suddenly those from the wild zones rose from that zone and struck at the vertical city that had previously been invisible. The wild and safe zones collided in the sky above New York in a manner no one in the safe zones had predicted. Of course, the zones also collide in Saudi Arabia, where the USA's obsession with cheap petrol for one-third of the world's cars has generated the unholy alliance between American power and Saudi oil wealth.

Moreover, the events of 11 September are the most dramatic example so far of a non-territorial network war or 'netwar' involving some novel forms taken by the 'multitude'. And hierarchies have great difficulty fighting such networks. Indeed, networks are best at fighting those engaged in netwars (see Arquilla and

Ronfeldt 2001: 17). Al-Qaida has been likened to a self-organizing system 'on the edge of chaos'. The 'amorphousness of al-Qaida not only makes it difficult to hunt down its members and pin blame on individuals: it also means it does not necessarily have the same form from day to day, a clear beginning or end' (Meek 2001). Indeed, 'what they receive from Bin Laden and his associates is less specific orders and training than a clear, simple ideology, which they are expected to go out into the world and put into practice on their own' (Meek 2001). This emergent global fluid of international terrorism is hard to defeat because it is made up of very different self-organizing elements. They regularly change their shape, form and activities. Such mutating capacity renders them 'invisible' if on occasions awesomely present.

Castells (2001) describes the nature of 'non-linear' warfare that occurs against such an 'enemy'. It eliminates the notion of a military front line through 'swarming'. Such swarming involves small autonomous units possessing high fire power, very rapid mobility, robust communications, real-time information and a capacity to 'sense' the enemy. This 'non-linear warfare represents a high-tech version of the old tradition of guerrilla struggles. This "network-centric" warfare . . . is entirely dependent upon robust, secure communication, able to maintain constant connection between the nodes of an all-channel network' (Castells 2001: 161–2; Duffield 2001: 14).

I have thus suggested that, rather than there being *an* 'Empire' with 'its' multitude, there is what we might hypothesize as a new attractor. This could be designated as 'societies as empires'. Societies across the world are being drawn into developing as 'empire'. And, as they are drawn into such an attractor, so new, unstable and unpredictable multitudes arise, seeking to topple those empires and their icons. Societies as empires are developing some strange new practices as systems develop to deal with the non-linear multitudes that are increasingly in their very midst.

Cosmopolitanism

But there is something else going on here within the emergent system of global complexity. Let me return briefly to when there was a 'simple' system of hierarchical nation states. When the world consisted of nation states, the 'other' society was almost always something to fear, to attack, to colonize, to dominate and to keep at bay. The other was dangerous, especially others on the move, such as armies, migrants, traders, vagrants, travellers who might stay. Citizenship came to consist of rights attributable to tightly specified categories of those who were unambiguously within *and* part of the 'society'. This system of national societies involved massive antagonism towards the other, with relationships normally being 'nasty, brutish and short' (see Diken 1998).

But we should consider here whether a 'cosmopolitan' global fluid is uncertainly and contingently emerging (D. Harvey 2000). Is a set of 'global' values and dispositions becoming an emergent and irreversible implication of global complexity? Are 'societies' increasingly forming themselves *within* such an evolving complex and will they be subject to scandalized disapproval if they do not display cosmopolitanism upon the global screen? Is the 'enemy' for each society as empire the global risks that have few borders or boundaries and that can be as much within the society as without? These risks include asylum-seekers, terrorists, diseases and viruses, environmental and health risks (see Van Loon 2002). Such a cosmopolitan fluid involves various characteristics (see Waldron 1995; Tomlinson 1999; Beck 2000; Cwerner 2000; Franklin et al. 2000; Walby 2001).

1 There is extensive *mobility* where people have the right to 'travel' corporeally, imaginatively and virtually and, for significant numbers of workers, students, tourists, asylum-seekers and so on, the means to travel and to consume places, peoples, rights and environments *en route*.

2 There is a *curiosity* about places, peoples and cultures and a rudimentary capacity to 'map' one's own society and its culture in terms of history and geography. There is a stance of *openness* to other peoples and cultures and a willingness/ability to value elements of the language/culture/history of multiple, contested and fragmented 'others' to one's own culture, provided that they meet certain global standards.

3 There is a willingness to take *risks* by virtue of encountering various 'others', combined with a *semiotic* skill to interpret and

evaluate images of other natures, places and societies, to see what they are meant to represent, and to know when they are ironic.

4   There are some global *standards* by which other places, cultures and people are positioned and can be judged. Many international organizations following the founding of the UN advocate and promulgate such standards.

Two writers that articulated the notion of the cosmopolitan are Salman Rushdie and C. L. R. James. Rushdie wrote in 1990: 'If *The Satanic Verses* is anything, it is a migrant's-eye view of the world. It is written from the very experience of uprooting, disjuncture and metamorphosis . . . that is the migrant condition, and from which, I believe, can be derived a metaphor for all humanity' (cited in Waldron 1995: 93). And C. L. R. James once wrote: 'The relation of classes had to change before I discovered that it's not quality of goods and utility that matter, but movement, not where you are or what you are, but where you come from, where you are going and the rate at which you are getting there' (cited in Clifford 1992: 96; see also Clifford 1997).

Such an emergent global fluid stems from the intensively mediated relations now swarming the world. This is even true in mainland China where the massive growth of diverse media is generating a recosmopolitanism (Ong and Nonini 1997; Yang 1997). The UN Commission on Global Governance (1995), set up to report on the first fifty years of the UN, talks of 'Our Global Neighbourhood', arguing that a mediated, enforced global proximity is generating cosmopolitanism (see also Tomlinson 1999: ch. 6; Beck 2000). Nelson Mandela often refers to 'the people of South Africa and the world who are watching' on their TV screens (UN Commission on Global Governance 1995: 107). The 'we' in Mandela's speeches almost always evokes those beyond South Africa that view South Africa upon the global media and have collectively participated in the country's rebirth through an enforced televisual proximity. When Mandela states that 'we are one people', he is pointing both to South Africa and to the rest of the world that is witnessing. Likewise the pointing from the TV commentators to the collective 'we' at Princess Diana's funeral was to the astonishing 2.5 billion people witnessing and sharing on the global screen, as the iconic 'global healer' was sanctified by the whole world (Richards et al. 1999: 3).

Indeed, since the fall of the Berlin Wall in 1989, there have been various 'global events' when *The Whole World is Watching* (Gitlin 1980). On 11 September 2001, the whole world watched the surreal and stranger-than-Hollywood moment when live planes with live passengers flew into and demolished two of the largest buildings in the world. The World Trade Center, with up to 150,000 workers and visitors, a city in the air, was at two strokes bombed out of existence with the whole world agog. The hugely unlikely forming of a 'global coalition against terrorism' both depended upon such collective watching and helped to promote further the cosmopolitan fluid. Collective global disasters are the key to the forming of such cosmopolitan global fluids, perhaps beginning with the founding moment of the Nuremberg trials in the immediate post-Second World War period.

Moreover, various visual representations of the earth or globe increasingly challenge the importance of 'national' flags (see Ingold 1993; Cosgrove 1994). The iconic blue globe involves seeing the earth in dark space, as a whole defined against threatening emptiness, with no lines or political colouring, freezing a moment in time. The globe functions as a symbol of authority, organization, and coverage of global information, particularly in news programmes.

More generally, images of space are often used to connote the endless possibilities of travel and the potential 'cosmopolitan' consumption of other places and cultured from all across the globe (Urry 2000b: ch. 7). Hebdige concludes that a 'mundane cosmopolitanism' is part of many people's everyday experience, as they are world travellers, both corporeally and through the TV in their living room: 'It is part of being "taken for a ride" in and through late-20th century consumer culture. In the 1990s everybody [at least in the West] is more or less cosmopolitan' (1990: 20).

A powerful 'televisual flow' throws viewers into the flowing visual world lying beyond the domestic regime. There is an instantaneous mirror reflecting the cultures of the rest of the world that are mirrored into people's homes (Williams 1974; Allan 1997; Hoskins 2001). Arundhati Roy evocatively describes an elderly woman whose life is transformed by the instantaneous and often 'live' visual perception of multiple 'global others'. Roy writes: 'She presided over the World in her drawing room on satellite TV. . . . It happened overnight. Blondes, wars, famines, football, sex, music, coups d'état – they all arrived on the same train. They unpacked together. They stayed at the same hotel . . . whole wars, famines, picturesque massacres and Bill Clinton could be summoned up like servants' (1997: 27). There is thus a hugely diverse and changing array of 'reference groups' that is disclosed and exposed especially through TV and now the Internet. The 'cosmopolitan traveller' may derive ideas, values, norms and senses of justice from an incredible array of such sources (Waldron 1995; Walby 2001).

Such sensations of other places can create an awareness of cosmopolitan interdependence and a 'panhumanity' (Franklin et al. 2000). The flows of information, knowledge, money, commodities, people and images 'have intensified to the extent that the sense of spatial distance which separated and insulated people from the need to take into account all the other people which make up what has become known as humanity has become eroded' (Featherstone 1993: 169). By participating in the practice of consuming in and through the media, people experience themselves as part of a dispersed, global civicness, sharing similar experiences and united by the sense at least that they are witnessing the world and its mosaic of cultures with millions of dispersed others (Gitlin 1980; Dayan and Katz 1992).

Acording to the UN, this global civicness is generating some sense of the universal standards by which human development is to be judged (see UNDP 2000). One paradoxical consequence of global complexity is to provide the context in which universal rights, a panhumanity, relating not only to humans but also to animals and environments, comes to constitute a framing for collective action. Illustrations of such panhumanity are the wide range of what we can call 'global gift giving', the giving to distant (unknown) others of money, time, objects, software and information (via mega events like Liveaid, via local events or via the Internet).

Cosmopolitanism should be seen as produced by, and further elaborating, the glocalization attractor through transforming relations *between* the global and the local (Tomlinson 1999: 194–207). The drawing of many 'localities' into the attractor of 'glocality' provides preconditions for emergence: 'changes in our actual physical environments, the routine factoring in of distant political-economic processes into life-plans, the penetration of our homes by new media and communications technology, multiculturalism as increasingly the norm, increased mobility and foreign travel, even the effects of "cosmopolitanizing" of food culture' (Tomlinson 1999: 199–200; see also Rotblat 1997b; Beck 2000).

Thus the apparently local and the apparently cosmopolitan should not necessarily be counterposed. Powerful sets of dispositions in the contemporary world are neither localist and proximate nor global and universal. As Zygmunt Bauman argues in *Liquid Modernity* via a discussion of Derrida's to 'think travel': 'the trick is to be at home in many homes, but to be in each inside and outside at the same time, to combine intimacy with the critical look of an outsider, involvement with detachment' (2000: 207). Cosmopolitan fluidity thus involves the capacity to live simultaneously in *both* the global and the local, in the distant and proximate, in the universal and the particular. Such cosmopolitanism involves comprehending the specificity of one's local context, to connect to other locally specific contexts and to be responsive to the complex threats and opportunities of a globalizing world. We can thus talk of a 'glocalized cosmopolitanism' in which 'in the everyday lifestyle choices they make, cosmopolitans need routinely to experience the wider world as touching their local lifeworld, and vice versa' (Tomlinson 1999: 198).

Such cosmopolitanism as a global fluid appears increasingly widespread through the 'shrinking world' of various intersecting global fluids that were outlined in chapter 4. Its increasing scale and complex impact will irreversibly transform each civil society, altering the conditions under which 'social actors assemble, organize, and mobilize' (Cohen and Arato 1992: 151). And, as they assemble, organize and mobilize differently, so new, unpredictable and emergent cosmopolitan identities, practices and cognitive praxes will emerge (Eyerman and Jamison 1991). Out of TV and jet travel, the mobile and the modem, there is an emergent global fluid of cosmopolitanism. This transforms what it is that appears to be co-present and what is mediated, what is embodied and what is distant, what is local and what is global (D. Harvey 2000: 85–6).

The emergence of the cosmopolitan global fluid thus shows the irreversible, unpredictable and chaotic workings of global complexity. And complexity theory seems to provide the means to examine how cosmopolitanism has come to develop as a new emergent fluid of global ordering.

Conclusion

John Gray (2001) describes the current state of the globe as 'an intractably disordered world'. I have tried to show that 'complexity' provides a wide array of metaphors, concepts and theories essential for examining such intractable disorderliness. Relations across that world are complex, rich and non-linear, involving multiple negative and, more significantly, positive feedback loops. There are ineluctable patterns of increasing returns and long-term path dependencies. Such global systems, or regions, GINs and GFs, are characterized by unpredictability and irreversibility; they lack any finalized 'equilibrium' or 'order'. They do not exhibit and sustain unchanging structural stability. Complexity elaborates how there is order *and* disorder within all physical and social systems. Following Gray we can see how there is a complex world, unpredictable and irreversible, disorderly but not simply anarchic.

Such complexity derives from what I have described as the dialectic of moorings *and* mobilities. If, to express this far too simply, the social world were to be entirely moored or entirely mobile, then systems would not be dynamic and complex. But social life seems to be increasingly constituted through material worlds that involve new and distinct moorings that enable, produce and presuppose extensive new mobilities. So many more systems are complex, strangely ordered, with new shapes moving in and through time–space.

In such systems the various components are irreversibly drawn towards various 'attractors' that exercise a gravity effect. Such components within any system operate under conditions that are far from equilibrium, partly because each responds to 'local' sources of information. But components at one location have substantial time–space effects elsewhere through multiple connections and awesome trajectories. Such systems possess a history that irreversibly evolves and where past events are not 'forgotten'. Points of bifurcation are reached when the system branches, since 'causes' and 'effects' are disproportionate. There are non-linear relationships between them, with the consequence that systems can move quickly and dramatically from one state to another. Systems 'tip' or 'turn', especially those that are organized through 'networked' relationships that usher in some surprising and distinct effects.

Finally, let me consider briefly here how this connects to the theory of 'reflexive modernization'. It has been argued that 'social structures, national in scope, are being displaced by such global information and communication (I and C) structures' (Lash and Urry 1994: 6). These emergent systems of information and communication are the bases for increased reflexivity. Through the increasingly structural power of information and communications the 'structure' of 'societies' has progressively less purchase.

And there is heightened reflexivity produced by and through these new 'I and C' structures. Reflexive modernization characterizes social life in which individuals and systems reflexively monitor especially the side effects of modernity. Such reflexivity moreover gives rise to many new structures, especially of various expert systems. Such reflexivity is, however, cultural as well as cognitive (see Lash and Urry 1994; Waldron 1995). It is not only a matter of scientific or expert systems that enable the side effects of the modern to be monitored, organized around and in cases rectified. Rather, reflexive modernization involves aesthetic-expressive systems that result in huge new cultural industries, a veritable economy of signs.

I want though to suggest that these processes of reflexive modernization stem from what I have described as the emergent global fluid of the cosmopolitan. Cosmopolitanism provides dispositions of an appropriate cultural reflexivity within emergent global complexities. The form now taken by reflexive modernization is the global fluid of cosmopolitanism. Such a cosmopolitan fluid involves redrawing the speed of the global *and* the slowness of the ontologically grounded. It irreversibly transforms the conditions under which other networks and fluids operate as well as what have been historically understood as 'societies'. This connects to the shift that Lash describes as the move from the risk society, as examined by Beck, to the more general risk culture (Beck 1992, 1998; Lash 2000). Such a risk culture has to deal with risks that unambiguously run across borders. These include post-industrial risks, especially involved in informational flows (biotechnology, cybersurveillance, epidemics, waste products, GM foods, cyber-crime, international terrorism), as well as with the risk taking that is part of the very processes of innovation (Van Loon 2002). And, corresponding to this shift is a corresponding shift from national society to the increasing power of a cosmopolitan global fluid, from modernity to reflexive modernization, as others have expressed this.

And we might further see complexity theories as deriving from and in turn enhancing cosmopolitanism. This global fluid, with many convergent, overlapping and irreversible interdependencies with other networks and fluids, serves to remake social relations across the world, but not in a linear, closed and finalized form. Complexity is the theory that cosmopolitanism produces and generalizes, that captures and reflects the *systemic* features of powerful material worlds.

Thus cosmopolitanism involves an emergent global fluid that will in part reconfigure how the social sciences develop in a post-societal era of global complexity. It will lead to the spread of the-ories of global complexity as one of the major means of capturing, representing and performing the new world ordering that remains balancing 'on the edge of chaos'. Complexity theories themselves seem irreducibly part of the emergent systems *of* global com-plexity. Thus we are going with the flow, so to speak, if we develop, as I have tried to here, the implications of the complex-ity sciences for the many global systems currently haunting the world's population.

References

Abbott, A. 2001. *Time Matters*. Chicago: University of Chicago Press.

Adam, B. 1990. *Time and Social Theory*. Cambridge: Polity.

Adam, B. 1998. *Timescapes of Modernity*. London: Routledge.

Adam, B. 2000. 'The temporal gaze: The challenge for sociological theory in the context of GM foods', *British Journal of Sociology*, 51: 125–42.

Adam, B., Beck, U., and van Loon, J. (eds) 2000. *The Risk Society and Beyond*. London: Sage.

Adams, J. 1995. *Risk*. London: UCL Press.

Albrow, M. 1996. *The Global Age*. Cambridge: Polity.

Allan, S. 1997. 'Raymond Williams and the culture of televisual flow', in J. Wallace and S. Nield (eds), *Raymond Williams Now: Knowledge, Limits and the Future*. London: Macmillan.

Anderson, A. 1997. *Media, Culture and the Environment*. London: UCL Press.

Appadurai, A. 1990. 'Disjuncture and difference in the global cultural economy', *Theory, Culture and Society*, 7: 295–310.

Appadurai, A. 1996. *Modernity at Large*. Minneapolis: Minneapolis University Press.

Archer, M. 1995. *Realist Social Theory*. Cambridge: Cambridge University Press.

Arquilla, J., and Ronfeldt, D. 2001. 'The advent of netwars (revisited)', in J. Arquilla and D. Ronfeldt (eds), *Networks and Netwars*. Santa Monica: Rand.

Arthur, B. 1994a. *Increasing Returns and Path Dependence in the Economy*. Ann Arbor: University of Michigan Press.

Arthur, B. 1994b. 'Summary Remarks', in G. Cowan, D. Pines and D. Meltzer (eds), *Complexity, Metaphors, Models and Reality*. Santa

Fe Institute: Studies in the Sciences of Complexity Proceedings, vol. 19.

Augé, M. 1995. *Non-Places*. London: Verso.

Bachelard, G. 1942/1983. *Water and Dreams: An Essay on the Imagination of Matter*. Farrell, Dallas: Pegasus.

Baker, P. 1993. 'Chaos, order, and sociological theory', *Sociological Inquiry*, 63: 123–49.

Bales, K. 1999. *Disposable People: New Slavery in the Global Economy*. Berkeley and Los Angeles: University of California Press.

Balkin, J. 1999. 'How mass media simulate political transparency', *Cultural Values*, 3: 393–413.

Barber, B. 1996. *Jihad vs McWorld*. New York: Ballantine.

Baudrillard, J. 1983. *Simulations*. New York: Semiotext(e).

Bauman, Z. 2000. *Liquid Modernity*. Cambridge: Polity.

Beck, U. 1992. *Risk Society*. London: Sage.

Beck, U. 1998. *World Risk Society*. Cambridge: Polity.

Beck, U. 2000. 'The cosmopolitan perspective: On the sociology of the second age of modernity', *British Journal of Sociology*, 51: 79–106.

Bhabha, H. 1992. 'Double Visions', *Artforum*. January: 82–90.

Biggs, M. 1998. 'Collective mobilization as self-reinforcing process: The organization of Chicago's working class in 1886', Harvard–Oxford–Stockholm Sociology Conference, April.

Billig, M. 1995. *Banal Nationalism*. London: Sage.

Boden, D. 2000. 'Worlds in action: Information, instantaneity and global futures trading', in B. Adam, U. Beck, U. and J. van Loon (eds), *The Risk Society and Beyond*. London: Sage.

Boden, D., and Molotch, H. 1994. 'The compulsion to proximity', in R. Friedland and D. Boden (eds), *Nowhere: Space, Time and Modernity*. Berkeley, California: University of California Press.

Bogard, W. 1996. *The Simulation of Surveillance*. Cambridge: Cambridge University Press.

Bogard, W. 2000. 'Simmel in cyberspace: Strangeness and distance in postmodern communications', *Space and Culture*, 4/5: 23–46.

Brand, S. 1999. *The Clock of the Long Now*. London: Phoenix.

Braudel, F. 1973. *Capitalism and Material Life, 1400–1800*. New York: Harper & Row.

Brenner, N. 1997. 'Global, fragmented, hierarchical: Henri Lefebvre's geographies of globalization', *Public Culture*, 10: 135–68.

Brenner, N. 1999a. 'Beyond state-centrism? Space, territoriality, and geographical scale in globalization studies', *Theory and Society*, 28: 39–78.

Brenner, N. 1999b. 'Globalisation as reterritorialisation: The re-scaling of urban governance in the European Union', *Urban Studies*, 36: 431–51.

Brunn, S., and Leinbach, R. (eds) 1991. *Collapsing Space and Time: Geographic Aspects of Communications and Information*. London: HarperCollins.

Budiansky, S. 1995. *Nature's Keepers*. London: Weidenfeld and Nicolson.

Burt, R. 1992. *Structural Holes*. Cambridge, Mass.: Harvard University Press.

Butler, J. 1993. *Bodies the Matter*. London: Routledge.

Byrne, D. 1997. 'Chaotic places or complex places', in S. Westwood and J. Williams (eds), *Imagining Cities*. London: Routledge.

Byrne, D. 1998. *Complexity Theory and the Social Sciences*. London: Routledge.

Cairncross, F. 1998. *The Death of Distance*. London: Orion.

Capra, F. 1996. *The Web of Life*. London: HarperCollins.

Capra, F. 2002. *The Hidden Connections: A Science for Sustainable Living*. London: HarperCollins.

Castells, M. 1996. *The Information Age*, i. *The Rise of the Network Society*. Oxford: Blackwell.

Castells, M. 1997. *The Information Age*, ii. *The Power of Identity*. Oxford: Blackwell.

Castells, M. 1998. *The Information Age*, iii. *End of Millennium*. Oxford: Blackwell.

Castells, M. 2000. 'Materials for an explanatory theory of the network society', *British Journal of Sociology*, 51: 5–24.

Castells, M. 2001. *The Internet Galaxy*. Oxford: Oxford University Press.

Casti, J. 1994. *Complexification*. London: Abacus.

Chase-Dunn, C., Kawano, Y., and Brewer, B. 2000. 'Trade globalisation since 1795: Waves of integration in the world-system', *American Sociological Review*, 65: 77–95.

Cilliers, P. 1998. *Complexity and Post-Modernism*. London: Routledge.

Clark, N. 2000. '"Botanizing on the asphalt"? The complex life of cosmopolitan bodies', *Body and Society*, 6: 13–34.

Clifford, J. 1992. 'Travelling cultures', in L. Grossberg et al. (eds), *Cultural Studies*. Berkeley and Los Angeles: University of California Press.

Clifford, J. 1997. *Routes*. Cambridge, Mass.: Harvard University Press.

Cohen, J., and Arato, A. 1992. *Civil Society and Political Theory*. Cambridge, Mass., and London: MIT Press.

Cohen, J., and Stewart, I. 1994. *The Collapse of Chaos*. Harmondsworth: Penguin.

Cohen, R. 1997. *Global Diasporas*. London: UCL Press.

Cohen, S. 2001. *States of Denial*. Cambridge: Polity.

Colborn, T., Meyers, J., and Dumanoski, D. 1996. *Our Stolen Future: How*

Man-Made Chemicals are Threatening our Fertility, Intelligence and Survival. Boston: Little, Brown & Company.

Cosgrove, D. 1994. 'Contested global visions: One-world, whole-earth, and the Apollo space photographs', *Annals of the Association of American Geographers*, 84:270–94.

Coveney, P. 2000. 'A clash of doctrines: The arrow of time in modern physics', in P. Baert (ed.), *Time in Contemporary Intellectual Thought*. Amsterdam: Elsevier.

Coveney, P., and Highfield, R. 1990. *The Arrow of Time*. London: Flamingo.

Cwerner, S. 2000. 'The chronopolitan ideal: Time, belonging and globalization', *Time and Society*, 2/3: 331–45.

Davies, P. 2001a. 'Before the Big Bang', *Prospect*, June: 56–9.

Davies, P. 2001b. *How to Build a Time Machine*. London: Allen Lane.

Davis, M. 2000a. *Ecology of Fear*. London: Picador.

Davis, M. 2000b. *Magical Urbanism*. London: Verso.

Dayan, D., and Katz, E. 1992. *Media Events: The Live Broadcasting of History*. Cambridge, Mass.: Harvard University Press.

De Landa, M. 1997. *A Thousand Years of Nonlinear History*. New York: Swerve.

Delanty, G. 2000. *Citizenship in a Global Age*. Buckingham: Open University Press.

Deleuze, G., and Guattari, F. 1986. *Nomadology*. New York: Semiotext(e).

Deleuze, G., and Guattari, F. 1988. *A Thousand Plateaus: Capitalism and Schizophrenia*. London: Athlone Press.

Dicken, P., Kelly, P., Old, K., and Yeung, H. 2001. 'Chains and networks, territories and scales: Towards a relational framework for analysing the global economy', *Global Networks*, 1: 89–112.

Diken, B. 1998. *Strangers, Ambivalence and Social Theory*. Aldershot: Ashgate.

Dillon, M. 2000. 'Poststructuralism, complexity and poetics', *Theory, Culture and Society*, 17: 1–26.

Dionne, E. 1998. 'Swoosh: Public shaming nets results', *International Herald Tribune*, 15 May, 11.

Duffield, M. 2001. *Global Governance and the New Wars*. London and New York: Zed Books.

Durkheim, E. 1915/1968. *The Elementary Forms of the Religious Life*. London: George Allen & Unwin.

Eatwell, J., and Taylor, L. 2000. *Global Finance at Risk*. New York: New Press.

Eco, U. 1986. *Travels in Hyper-Reality*. London: Picador.

Elster, J. 1985. *Making Sense of Marx*. Cambridge: Cambridge University Press.

Emirbayer, M. 1997. 'Manifesto for a relational sociology', *American Journal of Sociology*, 103: 281–317.

Emirbayer, M., and Mische, A. 1998. 'What is agency?', *American Journal of Sociology*, 103: 962–1023.

Eve, R., Horsfall, S., and Lee, M. (eds) 1997. *Chaos, Complexity, and Sociology*. Thousand Oaks, Calif.: Sage.

Eyerman, R., and Jamison, A. 1991. *Social Movements: A Cognitive Approach*. Cambridge: Polity.

Featherstone, M. 1993. 'Global and local cultures', in J. Bird et al. (eds), *Mapping the Futures: Local Cultures, Global Change*. London: Sage.

Featherstone, M. 2000. 'Archiving cultures', *British Journal of Sociology*, 51: 161–84.

Foucault, M. 1977. *Discipline and Punish*. London: Allen Lane.

Fox Keller, E. 1985. *Reflections on Gender and Science*. New Haven: Yale University Press.

Francis, R. 1993. 'Chaos, order, sociological theory: a comment', *Sociological Theory*, 63: 239–42.

Franklin, S., Lury, C., and Stacey, J. 2000. *Global Nature, Global Culture*. London: Sage.

Friedman, T. 2000. *The Lexus and the Olive Tree*. London: Harper.

Fukuyama, F. 1992. *The End of History and the Last Man*. Harmondsworth: Penguin.

Game, A. 1998. 'Travel', *International Sociology*, 13: 41–58.

Gates, B. 1999. *Business @ the Speed of Thought*. Harmondsworth: Penguin.

Giddens, A. 1984. *The Constitution of Society*. Cambridge: Polity.

Giddens, A. 1990. *The Consequences of Modernity*. Stanford, Calif.: Stanford University Press.

Giddens, A., and Hutton, W. 2000. 'Anthony Giddens and Will Hutton in conversation', in W. Hutton and A. Giddens (eds), *On the Edge. Living with Global Capitalism*. London: Jonathan Cape.

Gilbert, N. 1995. 'Emergence in social simulation', in N. Gilbert and R. Conte (eds), *Artificial Societies*. London: UCL Press.

Gille, Z. 2000. 'Cognitive cartography in a European wasteland', in M. Burawoy et al. (eds), *Global Ethnography*. Berkeley and Los Angeles: University of California Press.

Gitlin, T. 1980. *The Whole World is Watching*. Berkeley and Los Angeles: University of California Press.

Gladwell, M. 2000. *Tipping Points: How Little Things can Make a Big Difference*. Boston: Little, Brown & Company.

—— 2002. *The Tipping Point*, Boston: Black Bay Books.

Gleick, J. 1988. *Chaos*. London: Sphere.

Goerner, S. 1994. *Chaos and the Evolving Ecological Universe*. Amsterdam: Gordon & Breach.

Goldman, P., and Papson, S. 1998. *Nike Culture: The Sign of the Swoosh*. London: Sage.

Goldthorpe, J. 2000. *On Sociology*. Oxford: Oxford University Press.

Graham, S., and Marvin, S. 2001. *Splintering Urbanism*. London: Routledge.

Granovetter, M. 1983. 'The strength of weak ties: A network theory revisited', *Sociological Theory*, 1: 203–33.

Gray, J. 2001. 'The era of globalisation is over', *New Statesman*, 24 September.

Habermas, J. 2001. *The Postnational Constellation*. Cambridge: Polity.

Hardt, M., and Negri, A. 2000. *Empire*. Cambridge, Mass.: Harvard University Press.

Harvey, D. 1996. *Justice, Nature and the Geography of Difference*. Oxford: Blackwell.

Harvey, D. 2000. *Spaces of Hope*. Edinburgh: Edinburgh University Press.

Harvey, P. 1996. *Hybrids of Modernity*. London: Routledge.

Hawken, P., Lovins, A., and Lovins, L. H. 1999. *Natural Capitalism*. London: Earthscan.

Hawking, S. 1988. *A Brief History of Time*. London: Bantam.

Hayles, N. K. (ed.) 1991. *Chaos and Order: Complex Dynamics in Literature and Science*. Chicago: University of Chicago Press.

Hayles, N. K. 1999. *How We Became Posthuman*. Chicago: University of Chicago Press.

Hebdige, D. 1990. 'Fax to the future', *Marxism Today*, January: 18–23.

Held, D., McGrew, A., Goldblatt, D., and Perraton, J. 1999. *Global Transformations*. Cambridge: Polity.

Helmreich, S. 2000. 'Life @ Sea: Networking people, polities, and Planet Earth through marine diversity and biotechnology', School of American Research Seminar, Santa Fe, New Mexico, April–May.

Hirst, P., and Thompson, G. 1996. *Globalization in Question*. Cambridge: Polity.

Hoskins, A. 2001. 'Mediating time: The temporal mix of television'. *Time and Society*, 10: 213–33.

Ignatieff, M. 2000. *Virtual War*. London: Chatto & Windus.

Imken, O. 1999. 'The convergence of virtual and actual in the Global Matrix', in M. Crang, P. Crang and J. May (eds), *Virtual Geographies*. London: Routledge.

Ingold, T. 1993. 'Globes and spheres: The topology of environment', in

K. Milton (ed.), *Environmentalism: The View from Anthropology*. London: Routledge.

Jasper, J. 1997. *The Art of Moral Protest: Culture, Biography and Creativity in Social Movements*. Chicago and London: University of Chicago Press.

Jervis, R. 1997. *System Effects*. Princeton: Princeton University Press.

Jessop, B. 2000. 'The crisis of the national spatio-temporal fix and the tendential ecological dominance of globalizing capitalism', *International Journal of Urban and Regional Research*, 24: 323–60.

Jordan, J. 1998. 'The art of necessity: The subversive imagination of anti-road protest and Reclaim the Streets', in G. McKay (ed.), *DiY Culture: Part and Protest in Nineties Britain*. London and New York: Verso.

Kaplan, C. 1996. *Questions of Travel*. Durham, UNCS: Duke University Press.

Kauffman, S. 1993. *The Origins of Order*. New York: Oxford University Press.

Keck, M., and Sikkink, K. 1998. *Activists beyond Borders*. Ithaca, NY: Princeton University Press.

Keil, L., and Elliott, E. (eds) 1996. *Chaos Theory in the Social Sciences*. Ann Arbor: University of Michigan Press.

Keil, R. 1998. 'Globalization makes states: Perspectives of local governance in the age of the world city', *Review of International Political Economy*, 5: 616–46.

Kelly, K. 1995. *Out of Control: The New Biology of Machines*. London: Fourth Estate.

Kelly, K. 1998. *New Rules for the New Economy*. London: Fourth Estate.

Kern, S. 1983. *The Culture of Time and Space, 1880–1914*. London: Weidenfeld & Nicolson.

King, A. 1996. 'Worlds in the city: Manhattan transfer and the ascendance of spectacular space', *Planning Perspectives*, 11: 97–114.

Klein, N. 2000. *No Logo*. London: Flamingo.

Klein, N. 2001. 'Reclaiming the Commons', *New Left Review. Second Series*, 9: 81–9.

Knorr-Cetina, K. 1997. 'Sociality with objects: Social relations in postsocial knowledge societies', *Theory, Culture and Society*, 14: 1–30.

Krugman, P. 1996. *The Self-Organizing Economy*. Cambridge, Mass.: Blackwell.

Kwa, C. 2002. 'Romantic and baroque conceptions of complex wholes in the sciences', in J. Law and A. Mol (eds), *Complexities: Social Studies of Knowledge Practices*, Durham, NC: Duke University Press.

Lash, S. 1999. *Another Modernity: A Different Rationality*. Oxford: Blackwell.

Lash, S. 2000. 'Risk culture', in B. Adam, U. Beck and J. van Loon (eds), *The Risk Society and Beyond*. London: Sage.

Lash, S., and Urry, J. 1987. *The End of Organized Capitalism*. Cambridge: Polity.

Lash, S., and Urry, J. 1994. *Economies of Signs and Space*. London: Sage.

Latour, B. 1993. *We Have Never Been Modern*. Hemel Hempstead: Harvester Wheatsheaf.

Latour, B. 1999. 'On recalling ANT', in J. Law and J. Hassard (eds), *Actor Network Theory and After*. Oxford: Blackwell/Sociological Review.

Latour, B. 2000. 'When things strike back: A possible contribution of "science studies" to the social sciences', *British Journal of Sociology*, 51; 107–24.

Law, J. 1994. *Organizing Modernity*. Oxford: Blackwell.

Law, J. 2000. 'Ladbroke Grove, or how to think about failing systems', Dept of Sociology, Lancaster University.

Law, J., and Hetherington, K. 1999. 'Materialities, spatialities, globalities', Dept of Sociology, Lancaster University.

Law, J., and Mol, A. 2000. 'Situating technoscience: an inquiry into spatialities', Dept of Sociology, Lancaster University.

Lefebvre, H. 1991. *The Production of Space*. Oxford: Blackwell.

Levitt, P. 2001. *The Transnational Villagers*. Berkeley and Los Angeles: University of California Press.

Leyshon, A., and Thrift, N. 1997. *Money/Space*. London: Routledge.

Lodge, D. 1983. *Small World*. Harmondsworth: Penguin.

Luhmann, N. 1990. *Essays on Self-Reference*. New York: Columbia University Press.

Luhmann, N. 1995. *Social Systems*. Stanford, Calif.: Stanford University Press.

Luke, T. 1995. 'New world order or neo-world orders: Power, politics and ideology in informationalizing glocalities', in M. Featherstone, S. Lash and R. Robertson (eds), *Global Modernities*. London: Sage.

Lukes, S. 1973. *Power: A Radical View*. London: Macmillan.

Lyotard, J.-F. 1991. *The Inhuman: Reflections on Time*. Cambridge: Polity.

Maasen, S., and Weingart, P. 2000. *Metaphors and the Dynamics of Knowledge*. London: Routledge.

McCarthy, A. 2001. *Ambient Television*. Durham and London: Duke University Press.

McCrone, D. 1998. *The Sociology of Nationalism*. London: Routledge.

McKay, G. 1998. *DiY Culture: Party and Protest in Nineties Britain*. London and New York: Verso.

Macnaghten, P., and Urry, J. 1998. *Contested Natures*. London: Sage.

Mahoney, J. 2000. 'Path dependence in historical sociology', *Theory and Society*, 29: 507–48.

Maier, C. 1994. 'A surfeit of memory? Reflections of history, melancholy and denial', *History and Memory*, 5: 136–52.

Majone, G. 1994. 'The rise of the regulatory state in Europe', *West European Politics*, 17: 77–101.

Majone, G. 1996. *Regulating Europe*. London: Routledge.

Makimoto, T., and Manners, D. 1997. *Digital Nomad*. Chichester: John Wiley.

Malpas, J., and Wickham, G. 1995. 'Governance and failure: On the limits of sociology', *Australian and New Zealand Journal of Sociology*, 31: 37–50.

Mann, M. 1997. 'Has globalization ended the rise of the nation-state?', *Review of International Political Economy*, 4: 472–96.

Martin, H.-P., and Schumann, H. 1997. *The Global Trap*. London: Zed.

Marx, K., and Engels, F. 1848/1952. *The Manifesto of the Communist Party*. Moscow: Foreign Languages.

Maturana, H. 1981. 'Autopoeisis', in M. Zeleny (ed.), *Autopoeisis: A Theory of Living Organization*. New York: North Holland.

Medd, W. 2000. 'Complexity in the Wild'. Ph.D. Dept of Sociology, Lancaster University.

Meek, J. 2001. 'Why the management of a Danish hearing-aid maker may hold the key to stopping Bin Laden', *Guardian*, 18 October.

Melucci, A. 1996. *Challenging Codes: Collective Action in the Information Age*. Cambridge: Cambridge University Press.

Menon, M. 1997. 'Effects of modern science and technology on relations between nations', in J. Rotblat (ed.), *World Citizenship: Allegiance to Humanity*. London: Macmillan.

Meyer, J., Boli, J., Thomas, G., and Ramirez, F. 1997. 'World society and the nation-state', *American Journal of Sociology*, 103: 144–81.

Meyerowitz, J. 1985. *No Sense of Place*. New York: Oxford University Press.

Mingers, J. 1995. *Self-Producing Systems*. New York: Plenum.

Mol, A., and Law, J. 1994. 'Regions, networks and fluids: Anaemia and social topology', *Social Studies of Science*, 24: 641–71.

Monbiot, G. 2000. *Captive State: The Corporate Takeover of Britain*. London: Macmillan.

Morse, M. 1998. *Virtualities*. Bloomington, Ind.: Indiana University Press.

Motavalli, J. 2000. *Forward Drive*. San Francisco: Sierra Club.

Mouzelis, N. 1995. *Sociological Theory*. London: Routledge.

Murdoch, J. 1995. 'Actor-networks and the evolution of economic forms: Combining description and explanation in theories of regulation, flexible specialisation, and networks', *Environment and Planning A*, 27: 731–57.

Negroponte, N. 1995. *Being Digital*. New York: Alfred A. Knopf.

Nguyen, D. 1992. 'The spatialisation of metric time', *Time and Society*, 1: 29–50.

Nicolis, G. 1995. *Introduction to Non-Linear Science*. Cambridge: Cambridge University Press.

North, D. 1990. *Institutions, Institutional Change and Economic Performance*. Cambridge: Cambridge University Press.

Ó Riain, S. 2000. 'Net-working for a living: Irish software developers in the global market place', in M. Burawoy et al. (eds), *Global Ethnography*. Berkeley and Los Angeles: University of California Press.

Ohmae, K. 1992. *The Borderless World*. London: Fontana.

Ong, A., and Nonini, D. (eds) 1997. *Ungrounded Empires*. London: Routledge.

Papastergiadis, N. 2000. *The Turbulence of Migration*. Cambridge: Polity.

Parsons, T. 1960. *Structure and Process in Modern Societies*. New York: Free Press.

Parsons, T. 1971. *The System of Modern Societies*. New Jersey: Prentice-Hall.

Pascoe, D. 2001. *Airspaces*. London: Reaktion Books.

Perkman, M. 2000. 'Euroregions: Strategies of institution-building in the new European polity'. Ph.D., Dept of Sociology, Lancaster University.

Perrow, C. 1999. *Normal Accidents*. Princeton: Princeton University Press.

Peters, T. 1992. *Liberation Management*. London: Macmillan.

Plant, S. 1997. *Zeros and Ones*. London: Fourth Estate.

Power, M. 1994. *The Audit Explosion*. London: Demos.

Prigogine, I. 1997. *The End of Certainty*. New York: Free Press.

Prigogine, I., and Stengers, I. 1984. *Order out of Chaos*. London: Heinemann.

Rapoport, A. 1997. 'The dual role of the nation state in the evolution of world citizenship', in J. Rotblat (ed.), *World Citizenship: Allegiance to Humanity*. London: Macmillan.

Rasch, W., and Wolfe, C. (eds) 2000. *Observing Complexity*. Minneapolis: University of Minnesota Press.

Reed, M., and Harvey, D. 1992. 'The new science and the old: Complexity and realism in the social sciences', *Journal for the Theory of Social Behaviour*, 22: 353–80.

Rescher, N. 1998. *Complexity*. New Brunswick, NJ: Transaction Publishers.

Richards, J., Wilson, S., and Woodhead, L. (eds) 1999. *Diana: The Making of a Media Saint*. London: I. B. Tauris.

Rifkin, J. 2000. *The Age of Access.* Harmondsworth: Penguin.

Ritzer, G. 1992. *The McDonaldization of Society.* London: Pine Forge.

Ritzer, G. 1997. ' "McDisneyization" and "post-tourism": Complementary perspectives on contemporary tourism', in C. Rojek and J. Urry (eds), *Touring Cultures,* London: Routledge.

Ritzer, G. 1998. *The McDonaldization Thesis.* London: Sage.

Robertson, R. 1992. *Globalization: Social Theory and Global Culture.* London: Sage.

Roche, M. 2000. *Mega-Events and Modernity.* London: Routledge.

Roderick, I. 1997. 'Household sanitation and the flows of domestic space', *Space and Culture,* 1: 105–32.

Rojek, C., and Urry J. (eds) 1997. *Touring Cultures.* London: Routledge.

Ronfeldt, D. 2001. 'Social science at 190 mph on Nascar's biggest super-speedway', *First Monday* (firstmonday.org/issues/issue 5_2: 10 Sept. 2001).

Rose, N. 1996. 'Refiguring the territory of government', *Economy and Society,* 25: 327–56.

Rosenberg, J. 2000. *The Follies of Globalization Theory.* London: Verso.

Rotblat, J. 1997a. 'Preface, Executive Overview', in J. Rotblat (ed.), *World Citizenship: Allegiance to Humanity.* London: Macmillan.

Rotblat, J. (ed.) 1997b. *World Citizenship: Allegiance to Humanity.* London: Macmillan.

Roy, A. 1997. *The God of Small Things.* London: Flamingo.

Rushkoff, D. 1994. *Cyberia: Life in the Trenches of Hyperspace.* London: Flamingo.

Rycroft, R., and Kash, D. 1999. *The Complexity Challenge.* London: Pinter.

Sayer, A. 2000. 'System, lifeworld and gender: associational versus counterfactual thinking', *Sociology,* 34: 705–25.

Scannell, P. 1996. *Radio, Television and Modern Life.* Oxford: Blackwell.

Scholte, J. A. 2000. *Globalization: A Critical Introduction.* Basingstoke: Macmillan.

Shaw, M. 1994. *Global Society and International Relations: Sociological Concepts and Political Perspectives.* Cambridge: Polity.

Sheller, M. 2000. 'The mechanisms of mobility and liquidity: Re-thinking the movement in social movements', ISA/BSA Study Group on Protest and Social Movements, Manchester, November.

Sheller, M., and Urry, J. 2000. 'The city and the car', *International Journal of Urban and Regional Research,* 24: 737–57.

Sheller, M., and Urry J., forthcoming. 'Mobile transformations of "public" and "private" life', *Theory, Culture and Society,* 19.

Shields, R. 1997. 'Flow as a new paradigm', *Space and Culture,* 1: 1–4.

Shiva, V. 1989. *Staying Alive.* London: Zed.

Sklair, L. 2001. *The Transnational Capitalist Class.* Oxford: Blackwell.

Slater, D. 2001. 'Markets, materiality and the "new economy"', paper given to 'Geographies of New Economies' Seminar, Birmingham, UK, October.

Spencer, H. 1876/1893. *The Principles of Sociology,* i London: Williams & Norgate.

Stevenson, N. 1997. 'Globalization, national cultures and cultural citizenship', *Sociological Quarterly,* 38: 41–66.

Stewart, A. 2001. *Theories of Power and Domination.* London: Sage.

Stewart, I. 1989. *Does God Play Dice? The Mathematics of Chaos.* Oxford: Blackwell.

Stewart, P. 2001. 'Complexity theories, social theory, and the question of social complexity', *Philosophy of the Social Sciences,* 31: 323–60.

Strange, S. 1986. *Casino Capitalism.* Oxford: Blackwell.

Swyngedouw, E. 1992. 'Territorial organization and the space/technology nexus', *Transactions, Institute of British Geographers,* 17: 417–33.

Szerszynski, B. 1997. 'The varieties of ecological piety', *Worldviews: Environment, Culture, Religion,* 1: 37–55.

Szerszynski, B., and Urry, J. 2001. 'Visual citizenship?', in L. Short (ed.), *Cityshape, Landscape.* Carlisle: Carlisle College of Art and Design.

Thompson, J. 1995. *The Media and Modernity.* Cambridge: Polity.

Thompson, J. 2000. *Political Scandal: Power and Visibility in the Media Age.* Cambridge: Polity.

Thrift, N. 1999. 'The place of complexity', *Theory, Culture and Society,* 16: 31–70.

Thrift, N. 2001. *'The machine in the ghost: Software writing cities',* Hegemonies Conference, Centre for Science Studies, Lancaster University.

Tomlinson, J. 1999. *Globalization and Culture.* Cambridge: Polity.

UN Commission on Global Governance 1995. *Our Global Neighbourhood: The Report of the Commission on Global Governance.* Oxford: Oxford University Press.

UNDP 2000. *Human Development Report.* CD Rom. New York: UN.

Urry, J. 1990. *The Tourist Gaze.* London: Sage.

Urry, J. 1995. *Consuming Places.* London: Routledge.

Urry, J. 2000a. 'Mobile sociology', *British Journal of Sociology,* 51: 185–203.

Urry, J. 2000b. *Sociology beyond Societies.* London: Routledge.

Urry, J. 2001. *The Tourist Gaze.* 2nd edn. London: Sage.

Urry, J. 2002a. 'Globalizing the academy', in K. Robins and F. Webster (eds), *The Virtual University? Information, Markets and Managements.* Oxford: Oxford University Press.

Urry, J. 2002b. 'Mobility and proximity', *Sociology*, 36: 255–74.

Van Loon, J. 2002. *Risk and Technological Culture: Towards a Sociology of Virulence*. London: Routledge.

Volkmer, I. 1999. *News in the Global Sphere: A Study of CNN and its Impact on Global Communication*. Luton: University of Luton Press.

Walby, S. 1999. 'The new regulatory state: The social powers of the European Union', *British Journal of Sociology*, 50: 118–40.

Walby, S. 2001. 'From coalition to community: The politics of recognition as the handmaiden of the politics of redistribution', *Theory, Culture and Society*, 18: 113–35.

Walby, S. forthcoming. *Global Waves/National Pathways*. London: Sage.

Waldron, J. 1995. 'Minority cultures and the cosmopolitan alternative', in W. Kymlicka (ed.), *The Rights of Minority Cultures*. Oxford: Oxford University Press.

Waldrop, M. 1994. *Complexity*. London: Penguin.

Wallerstein, I. 1996. *Open the Social Sciences: Report of the Gulbenkian Commission on the Restructuring of the Social Sciences*. Stanford, Calif.: Stanford University Press.

Watson, J. 1997. 'Transnationalism, localization, and fast foods in East Asia', in J. Watson (ed.), *Golden Arches East*. Stanford, Calif.: Stanford University Press.

Watts, D. 1999. *Small Worlds*. Princeton: Princeton University Press.

Weiss, L. 1998. *The Myth of the Powerless State*. Cambridge: Polity.

Wellman, B. 2001. 'Physical space and cyberspace: The rise of personal networking', *International Journal of Urban and Regional Research*, 25: 227–52.

White, H. 1992. *Identity and Control*. Princeton: Princeton University Press.

White, H. 1995. 'Network switchings and Bayesian forks: Reconstructing the social and behavioural sciences', *Social Research*, 62: 1035–63.

Williams, R. 1973. *The Country and the City*. London: Chatto & Windus.

Williams, R. 1974. *Television: Technology and Cultural Form*. London: Fontana.

Williams, R. 1977. *Marxism and Literature*. Oxford: Oxford University Press.

WTO 2000. *World Tourism Organisation Database*. www.world-tourism.org.

Wynne, B. 1994. 'Scientific knowledge and the global environment', in M. Redclift and T. Benton (eds), *Social Theory and the Global Environment*. London: Routledge.

Yang, M. Mei-hui 1997. 'Mass media and transnational subjectivity in Shanghai: Notes on (re) cosmopolitanism in a Chinese metropolis', in A. Ong and D. Nonini (eds), *Ungrounded Empires*. London: Routledge.

Yuval-Davis, N. 1997. 'National Spaces and Collective Identities: Borders, Boundaries, Citizenship and Gender Relations'. Inaugural Lecture, University of Greenwich.

Zohar, D., and Marshall, I. 1994. *The Quantum Society*. New York: William Morrow.

Index

Index